P9-EMJ-473

Mordechai Nisan

AMERICAN
MIDDLE EAST
FOREIGN POLICY

A Political Reevaluation

Dawn Books
History in the Making

Published by
DAWN PUBLISHING COMPANY LTD.
17 Anselme Lavigne Blvd.,
Dollard des Ormeaux, Que.
H9A 1N3 / Canada

This book is set in 11 on 12 Times Roman

Legal Deposit — 3rd Quarter 1982
Dépôt légal — 3e trimestre 1982

ISBN: 0-9690001-1-1

Printed in Canada

CONTENTS

*For Irving Taitel
in friendship
and admiration*

PREFACE

The election of a new administration in Washington in 1980, under a new party banner and led by a new President, raised the possibility of a fundamental change in American foreign policy towards the Middle East region.

Under President Reagan, US policy is guided by a more conservative conception of political life, a more sober recognition of global threats, and a more traditional commitment to national principles than was the case in the past. This is not an easy time for the United States and there is no easy method to assure basic American interests in the Mideast zone. The near-permanent oil crisis, Soviet expansionism, warfare in Arab theaters from Lebanon to the Persian Gulf, and division within the Western alliance system —

have all left America grappling in darkness, and fire, without a guiding light. This essay is an effort to provide a light, a reasoned argument for a basic alteration in Washington's course, in order to rehabilitate America's position for its own welfare and the benefit of the Western World as a whole.

The crisis in US foreign policy in the region comes at a time when the realization of American goals is seen, more and more, dependent on the Arab world. Yet this stance is no longer credible and cannot be defended against the overwhelming evidence of recent years: the Arab world is *unable and unwilling* to cooperate with Washington's plan for achieving regional stability, the free flow of oil, and the elimination of Soviet penetration of the area. The theory of an American-Arab alignment is falsified by the facts. There is a variety of assymetries in their respective concerns and aspirations. This is the crisis in the United States foreign policy: the 'Arab paradigm' is ineffective and a new 'Israeli' one should be brought in for consideration.

The 'Israeli option' has been advanced from time to time, but never with the full force it merits. It constitutes a considerable transformation in the political conception of American policy in the Middle East. Fundamental beliefs are never easily rejected and new solutions often require much time to be accepted; thus, there is hardly an 'Israeli school of thought' in Washington political circles.

Nonetheless, a potentially very significant development took place in the American-Israeli relationship before President Reagan had yet completed his first year in office that suggested the desirability and applicability of the 'Israeli option'. In late 1981 the two countries signed a Memorandum of Understanding for Strategic Cooperation that indicated Washington's recognition of Israeli regional military value for American global concerns, and those of the Free World as a whole. Unfortunately, the tension in American-Israeli relations based, amongst other things, on the controversial AWACS issue was not at all eliminated by the strategic alliance between the two countries. Moreover, the Memorandum of Understanding seemed almost to be a tactical method of mollifying Israeli anxiety rather than an authentic expression of a mutual alliance system equally desired by both sides. The later American-Israeli dispute concerning Israel's formal annexation of the Golan Heights in December further disrupted the implementation of the strategic understanding.

The Reagan Administration, not unlike its predecessor, continued to move closer to the Arab camp with major diplomatic strides, if not leaps. The major landmarks in this political process were the following events:

1. *The Fahd Peace Plan of Saudi Arabia.* In August 1981, Crown Prince Fahd announced a peace plan which, on the one hand, called for the recognition of the PLO and the establishment of a PLO state and, on the other hand, ignored any specific mention of Israel or the need for the Arabs to conduct peace negotiations with her. In spite of these points, and the fact that the Saudis have consistently opposed the Camp David process that was initiated by the Americans, officials in Washington did not fail to express their positive impression of Fahd's plan. It has become fashionable, and not at all incorrect, to highlight the dangerous predominancy of Saudi Arabia in American political thinking on the Middle East. The loss of America's independent political will to direct national policy is not only counterproductive but grossly shameful as well.

It was interesting to witness the grotesque play of events following Senate approval in late October 1981 for Reagan's AWACS deal. This was passed against the opposition of major elements in American political life. Almost unbelievably, the following day the Saudis raised the price of their oil by $2.00 a barrel and cut production! Yet that display of Saudi arrogant behavior has not yet generated an American rethinking of its pro-Arab policy paradigm.

2. *The AWACS Arms Sale.* In October 1981, the American Administration was able to secure Senate approval for the sale of AWACS which

are known to be the most sophisticated recon-
naissance planes, sidewinder missiles, F-15 figh-
ter planes and other military material. This arms
package totalled $8.5 billion, the largest military
sale in American history. Israel had persistently
requested that America not undermine the regional military balance by supplying such weaponry to Saudi Arabia — unreliable for American
purposes and gravely hostile to Israel's existence.
Washington's willingness to support the Saudis
both militarily and diplomatically continued to
undermine Israel's confidence in her major
Western ally.

3. *The Sinai Multinational Force (MFO).* In October 1981, President Sadat of Egypt was as-
sassinated and, fearing the complete collapse of
the Camp David process, America urged and
continued to pressure Israel to complete the final
Israeli withdrawal scheduled for April 1982. Sadat's assassination suggested the fragility of the
Egyptian regime and Washington wanted Israel
to help President Mubarak to maintain his power
and the regime's policy orientation. All of this
became accentuated when four European countries — Britain, France, Holland, and Italy —
declared in November their readiness to send
forces to the MFO whose purpose is to monitor
the security situation between Israel and Egypt
following the final withdrawal. The Europeans
have always been totally opposed to the Ameri-
can-initiated Camp David process and this has

been harmful to American global status. In fact, their willingness to participate in the MFO was not meant to detract from their rejection of the peace which the MFO meant to serve. In their official statements the four European countries reiterated their support for the European community's Venice Declaration of June 1980 which calls for the recognition of the PLO and its participation in a final comprehensive Middle Eastern settlement. The Reagan administration exerted considerable pressure on the Israeli government to agree to Europe's participation notwithstanding the political contradiction regarding Camp David implicit in their participation. This escapade of diplomatic hypocrisy was designed to further satisfy the Arab world, assure Israel's final withdrawal, and indicate once again the pro-Arab orientation in Washington policy.

The Egyptians, Saudis, Jordanians, and other Arabs will likely continue to buy advanced weapon systems from the Americans but offer little in return. The American administration will expect Arab political support and military cooperation, though they will not be forthcoming. There is only one moral and practical policy for Washington to adopt. It must *first* establish a close strategic alliance with Israel and *then* encourage Arab countries to join such a Western-oriented bloc facing Soviet supported states in the Middle East. Only when this is done, and in the order outlined, can America expect to benefit from solid Arab support for its interests. As long as the Arabs can use Washington as a tool in their strategy against Israel, they shall undoubtedly do so. But this abuse of America must and can be stopped and then American honour will be restored in the region.

We should realistically move forward with a structure of peace that links together a core group of states within an American alliance system. The elements of such a vision include: Israel-Egyptian peace process, Israel-Jordanian peaceful coexistence, Israel-Christian Lebanese alliance, and Israel-Palestinian Arab normalization. At times, America has acted to disturb the degree of success achieved in these relationships. In particular we should note Washington's support for aspects of Egyptian intransigence, the possible U.S. sale of arms to Jordan that would undermine Israel's deterrent capacity, the abandonment of the Maronite Christians, and American flirtation with the PLO. The United States should solidify relationships of coexistence and not undermine them.

The American debate on foreign policy has not been polarized between an Israeli option and an Arab option because the major policy conception, supported by powerful political forces, has rested on Arab factors so heavily in the last decade. Yet the breakdown of that conception will force a debate on fundamentals and open the door to the adoption of a new policy pa-

radigm. Just when the sky seems to be falling in,
it is then that one's feet should be placed on solid
ground.

I have brought together discrete pieces of information and integrated them into a comprehensive political tapestry bearing on the legitimacy and solidity of an American-Israeli alliance. It has been my intention to avoid senti-
mentalism in this regard and concentrate on the
hard reality of such an alliance serving the joint
interests of the two countries, as well as Western
Europe. Indeed, it is petty emotionalism and irrational loyalties which have prevented the
search for an alternative American orientation in
the Mideast.

With an eye to the future, America will have to
draw upon its historic purpose and ponder its
political principles, assert its national will, and
prove its capacity for action in order to preserve
a modicum of order and balance in the Middle
East. To discover the authentic soul of America
is a precondition for the elucidation of a viable
foreign policy. That discovery, or rediscovery, is
an underlying motif of this essay. In all of this
the spark of true American pragmatism will have
to be lit: it is the application of an idea that is the
criterion of its value.

The gushing force of historical developments
will not stop in the 1980's, just as they did not
slow in the 1970's. It is therefore wise to take
stock of the state of affairs, to gain a perspective

on dominant political trends, and avoid being
blinded by individual events. This is a moment
for integrating facts and drawing general conclusions. In this sense, America and Israel together
may be successful in overcoming the winds of
fate and make history, so far as man is able.

Jerusalem,
Summer, 1982

Disintegration characterizes this time, and thus uncertainty: nothing stands firmly on its feet or on a hard faith in itself; one lives for tomorrow, as the day after tomorrow is dubious, and the ice that still supports us has become thin: all of us feel the warm, uncanny breath of the thawing wind; where we still walk, soon no one will be able to walk.

Friedrich Nietzsche,
The Will To Power, I, 2

CHAPTER 1:

POLITICS AND CIVILIZATION

If there is any validity to the dictum that 'knowledge is power', then it is perhaps logical to infer that a capacity for clear thinking and intelligent judgment must lay the basis for right political action. The king may not have to be a philosopher but he will, at least, need to have the requisite intellectual capacity to think well before acting. If we were to employ the language of Karl Deutsch we would refer to the learning capacity of a political system to incorporate new items of information at critical moments in order to carry out new policies to meet new conditions. The ability to adapt, improvise, and 'novelize' is a test of a government's preparedness to adjust to a changing, perhaps threatening, environment.

It is in this sense that the challenge emanating from the Middle East demands a new response from the United States. There are grave signs that the policies of America in that troubled region suffer from inadequate information, a closed communication network that inhibits varied and creative analysis of incoming data, and an unwillingness to test learning capacity by weighing the stated goals against external performance. The persistence of this situation can be veritably self-destructive. All flexibility and innovation have been eliminated from the system; little room is left for internal regeneration or external remedies. Idolizing the present format of policy and unable to humbly bow to incoming information is to worship 'strange gods' of moral hubris and intellectual rigidity. This is a sure formula for political failure, and perhaps national catastrophe.

The capacity of governments to change goals is a major test of their ability to adapt to new challenges. If the basis of a national goal is a fundamental value, it is not necessary to change values when goals are altered. The new goal is just a different means to realize the old value. Thus, goal-setting and goal-changing are *technical* tasks to be differentiated from the more *philosophic* task of value-determination. Yet, it is all too common for governments to turn the technical task of goal-setting into a philosophic category of a fixed value. This upsets the 'means-ends' dichotomy and, by consequence, freezes all maneuverability to alter policies to react successfully to new situations. Here too idol worship crushes human freedom.

Just as man's needs can be fulfilled in a variety of ways — one can eat three big meals a day or live on fourteen snacks, one can eat meat and other foods or survive as a vegetarian — so governments (man writ large) can adopt a multiple form of methods to achieve national goals. Capitalism may realize economic progress, or perhaps socialism will be more effective. At times military means are preferred means of policy; at other times economic or political means may be more effective. The functional viability and appropriateness of a method is its only realistic and rational justification. Blind commitment to a given goal, or means, is once again self-destructive of intellectual openness and political flexibility.

The United States, the most powerful nation bearing the mission of assuring democratic government and human liberty in the world, stands today facing a difficult and dangerous era in the 1980's. Much of mankind's fate in this decade will be affected by what happens in the Middle East. There the economic well-being of the Western World will be determined. There the strength of civilizational values against the onslaught of hostile forces will be tested. And there the maintenance of global stability against the threat of tension and war will be decided.

These challenges and dangers call for an American response that is forthright and grounded in a comprehensive understanding of the situation at hand. One may refer to the 'three circles' of policy concern that the U.S. administration must relate to, and certain flaws in thinking which have characterized American action until now.

1. The Soviet Union

Perhaps the best way to formulate the American misunderstanding regarding the USSR in the Mideast region is to suggest that even if nuclear parity was attainable and preserved between the super-powers, the geographical proximity of the Soviet Union to that strategic zone and its conventional military superiority would continue to threaten U.S. interests there.

Serious questions have been raised as to the viability of détente as a structure of stability between the two countries. The notion of 'peaceful coexistence' for the Soviet Union does not indicate the end of the internationalist thrust of Russian imperialism. Tension is not incompatible with détente but, rather, an inherent feature of an era in which Soviet ambitions are not advanced by outright warfare but by proxy conflicts, wars of 'national liberation', and assorted struggles to weaken Western positions beyond the North American-European periphery. Thus, peaceful coexistence turns out to be a form of the 'class struggle of socialism and capitalism in the world arena,' in the words of Soviet Minister of Foreign Affairs, Andrei Gromyko, echoing similar formulations by Brezhnev himself.[1] The clear implication for the Middle East is that Soviet efforts to further its goals there will not be deflected by superpower détente or peaceful coexistence. Rather, these notions act as a cover for continued interventionist strategies by the Kremlin.

Consistent with the USSR conception of détente as a tactical ploy is the continued emphasis on military priorities to realize national aims. Diplomacy and military strategy remain integrally linked in Soviet thinking and, when possible, practice.[2] This Clausewitzian approach utilizes diplomatic efforts to prepare the scene for military activism: it seeks to break up hostile coalitions and to neutralize potential enemies. The deadly relevance of this diplomatic strategy to the well-being of the NATO alliance is obvious, in an effort to prepare for a conventional Soviet thrust across Europe, a nuclear strike against the American mainland, or divide the West on critical Mideast issues.

Overall, it would be a grave misunderstanding to ignore the persistent confrontation orientation characteristic of Soviet policy embedded in a militaristic strategy intent on utilizing all di-

plomatic and warlike options to further extend
USSR power. This being the case the American
inclination, so typical of former National Security Adviser Brzezinski, of downplaying the Soviet
threat begins to sound very naive. Brzezinski has
paternalistically heeded the Soviets not to exploit
global unrest "in a short-sighted fashion".[3] A
year later in 1980 he lectured them on how irrelevant and counterproductive to their own interests would be the Russian "pursuit of outmoded
ideological objectives".[4] The hands are those of a
political actor, but the voice seems to be the professor's. Soviet activism in Angola and Mozam-
bique, interventionism in Ethiopia and Afghanistan, involvement in Lebanon and Iran, entrenchment in Southern Yemen, Libya, Syria
and Iraq — suggest that the Kremlin leaders do
not see such efforts as outmoded or short-
sighted, but riveted to the long-range strategic
purpose of expanding Soviet power and restrict-
ing and endangering Western interests. In these
efforts diplomacy works closely with military
methods, and the alleged restraint imposed by
détente and peaceful coexistence are shadows for
USSR conventional superiority operative under
the Russian nuclear umbrella. The US doctrine
of nuclear deterrence has proven vacuous; for
the Soviet Union deterrence has proven to be
effective in inhibiting a forthright American response to Russian threats.

Soviet actions seem to confirm that communist doctrine is still embedded in a vision of Russian expansionism, in the Mideast region and elsewhere. Brzezinski's insistence on trivializing the ideological gap between America and the USSR does not eliminate, however, the ongoing political reality. His persistent refusal to take seriously Soviet ambitions on a global level also does not deny their threatening portent for Western interests.

Some American observers, such as former US Ambassador to the United Nations Andrew Young, have suggested that the USSR is in the Middle East due to Arab frustration over the Palestinian issue which the Russians have pledged to try and solve. This view perceives in Soviet expansionist behavior a temporary political aberration or a psychological remedial motive. It is more realistic to see it as a *conscious strategic thrust* to extend Russian power in the most critical region of the world. In this context the 'Palestinian Problem' is an excuse — and a poor one — for a multi-purpose, independently-based Soviet policy. Soviet hegemonic expansionism may try to disguise its character under a moral cloak of aid to the 'poor Palestinians.' However, the naked form of *Realpolitik* imperialism cannot be hidden.

The American inability or unwillingness to understand the character of the Soviet regime, its policies and strategies, minimizes the possibility of generating an adequate American response in the Middle East. This is the first circle to claim the attention of US policy-makers in Washington.

2. The Arab World

A noted anthropologist, Edward Hall, has suggested that "in spite of over two thousand years of contact, Westerners and Arabs still do not understand each other".[5] What concerns us is whether it is legitimate to deduce a fundamental inability by the West, or America, to grasp the very different historical, cultural, and religious make-up of the Arab East based on repeated foreign policy failures in the Mideast. If it were in principle beyond the intellectual reach of the West to comprehend a very different Eastern reality, then American efforts are doomed in a deterministic fashion. This, however, contradicts the belief that man can learn and governments can improve their policy performance.

Still, the analyst must take account of repeated instances of a US failure to grasp the linguistic nuances in Arab expression and the deepest intentions underlying Arab political actions. Arab opposition and hostility to Israel have not been appreciated in their gravity by Americans. Prior to 1948 certain officials in the State Department held on to the unfounded conviction that in return for lots of Jewish money, King Ibn Saud would turn Saudi Arabia into a supporter of the Zionist dream. A more recent misunderstanding of Saudi views was recorded in a testimony by Senator Howard Baker. Following a visit to the oil-rich desert kingdom Baker reported that King Khalid said: "The solution to the Arab-Israeli conflict is very simple. We ask only that the Arabs may return to their homes and Israel return to its borders of 1967." Baker concluded: "The Arabs have learned to be moderate, reasonable. Gone are the days of Nasser's period when the Arabs threatened to exterminate the Israelis."[6] In the Arab code-language for the Mideast conflict, consistent with the political associations understood by all who are aware of the semantic keys to decode the cryptic messages, Khalid's formula for peace is a euphemism for Israel's destruction.[7] The return of the Arab refugees, innocently suggested, is the mechanism for a demographic revolution in Israel turning it into Arab Palestine. Linked to Israel's withdrawal to at least the '67 lines of territorial vulnerability —a 10-mile wide state! — the ultimate eradication of Israel becomes a matter of time. The naive, uninstructed American is caught in the mysterious, subtle web of Arab linguistic deception.

No doubt the major Arab feat in fooling the West in recent years was Sadat's "splendid strategic deception" in planning and executing the 1973 Yom Kippur War. American (and Israeli) intelligence services completely misread the signals of war emanating from Egypt and assumed

that his overall strategy was diplomatic negotia-
tion rather than military combat. Although the
outline of the plan for war was completed by
January 1973, Egypt initiated high-level contacts
with the U.S. administration in February to
create the impression of a willingness to seek a
political resolution of the Mideast deadlock. Sadat, in his autobiography, further reveals his
message to a foreign minister of a European
country of his intention to be at the UN General
Assembly session in October 1973.[8] All of this,
and more, was designed to blur Western perceptions and carry out the surprise attack against
Israel. This is a classic instance of underestimat-
ing Arab hostility to Israel and misunderstanding the manifold Arab uses of semantic and diplomatic devices to hide true intentions.

A specific instance of imputing peace convic-
tions when this is still very questionable concerns
the Egyptian decision to re-open the Suez Canal
in 1975. In 1976 Jesse Lewis, Jr., in a solid work
on American strategic bases in the Mediterranean, notes the Egyptian plan to "dig a tunnel
under the canal." He concludes by inferring that
this indicates that Egypt "does not want another
war with Israel," and that Sadat's real intention
is to revitalize the Canal zone.[9] In 1977, in an
interview to *Le Monde*, President Qaddafi of Libya divulged a conversation he held with Sadat in
Cairo on October 30, 1973. According to Qaddafi, Sadat told him that he was prepared to con-

clude any kind of peace with Israel in order to recover the Sinai Peninsula. But, Qaddafi continues,

> ...he added that he would extricate himself from his (peace) commitments to carry on the war against Israel once the Egyptian army was in a position to win a decisive victory. In the same context, he informed me that his project to construct a tunnel under the Suez Canal would —at the opportune moment — facilitate the deployment of Egyptian forces in the Sinai.[10]

In accord with that 1973 conversation, Sadat did in fact make a peace treaty with Israel and later as well, opened the canal. This record of carrying out the substance of the Sadat-Qaddafi conversation strengthens the Libyan's interpretation of the role of the tunnel compared to the American's interpretation. Of course, only the future will reveal whose interpretation is correct. Until then we can only assume that, as in the past, Qaddafi is a more reliable reporter and analyst of Sadat's hidden moves below the surface, in the deep recesses of the tunnel than the well-intentioned Jesse Lewis, Jr.

Indeed, Sadat inaugurated the first of five tunnels under the Suez Canal linking Egypt to Sinai in October 1980. At the opening ceremony Sadat declared that this is 'a new strategic event', as he boasted that 1,000 tanks can pass through the tunnel in one hour.

The recent radical changes taking place in Iran were hardly foreseen by American observers prior to changing the Mideast reality. A Congressional committee concluded in 1979 that "intelligence field reporting from Iran provided a narrow and cloudy window through which to observe the sweeping social and political changes underway."[11] The fall of the Shah, sparked by powerful opposition elements, was considered most unlikely. U.S. analysts did not realize that military hardware could not assure the survival of a segmented, divided political society threatened by far-reaching transformations in the nature of the regime (at least formally speaking). They also did not realize the force of religion in politics, particularly in a Moslem context.

A not dissimilar mistake was made in trying to comprehend the forces operative in the Lebanese Civil War. It was part of the common political wisdom of Western pundits to label that bitter struggle raging since 1975 a confrontation between 'PLO leftists and Christian rightists.' The usefulness of those terms in the age of 'semantic infiltration,' to borrow a phase from Daniel Moynihan, can no longer be taken seriously. Beyond any ideological rivalry over socio-economic questions, the fundamental causes of civil conflict between Muslim and Christian are rooted — (a) in an historical *religious* contest for national dominance, and (b) in an intrusion of *PLO* forces that upset the religious balance and undermined domestic stability in a country traditionally uninvolved in the regional Arab-Israeli conflict. The dichotomy of 'right-left' to grasp Lebanese turmoil in the '70's served to create the mistaken impression that, at least theoretically, peace could be realized by separating politics from religion and linking it to economics. That may be sober Western thinking in an American social context. In the Mideast it is misconceived from the start, with no finish in sight. It would be helpful to consider that the very different background and texture of political life in the Arab world compared to the West demands careful study by American policy-makers. Arab political language, diplomatic techniques, and military strategy will profoundly affect the ongoing Arab-Israeli conflict and the recent assertion of Muslim-Arab global power. This is the second circle for a renewed effort of American understanding and policy-articulation.

3. Israel

Since its creation in 1948, Israel has been overwhelmingly preoccupied with its national security imperatives as a sovereign state in a hostile region. The background of Jewish history and the contemporary experience of repeated warfare with the Arab states make of Israeli 'paranoia' a normative healthy state of mind. This basic concern for political existence in its most elemental form explains much of Israeli policy that Americans have, at times, misunderstood. When Donald McHenry, the U.S. Ambassador to the United Nations, tried to belittle Israeli anxiety by saying — on a visit to Jerusalem in March 1980 — 'I've had enough of that talk on security,' he perhaps failed to appreciate that Israeli security is not synonymous with Israeli grandeur, glory, or expansionism — but just survival.

The UN Security Council Resolution 242 has become over the years the focus of American diplomatic efforts to resolve the Mideast conflict. In fact, the Camp David Accords of 1978 explicitly built upon certain principles already enunciated in 242 from 1967. That resolution contains two critical clauses that seem incompatible with each other: (a) "the inadmissibility of the acquisition of territory by war", and (b) "respect for...territorial integrity and political independence of every state in the area and their right to live in peace within secure and recognized boundaries free from threats or acts of force."[12] The first clause implies that Israel is obligated to return all territories taken in the 1967 Six Day War from Egypt, Syria, and Jordan. The second clause implies, however, that it may be necessary to fix new boundaries — for Israel — that will accord it the territorial integrity and national security not available within her narrow, vulnerable pre-'67 frontiers.

The history of the conflict until 1967 does strongly suggest that Israel lacked the territorial depth to both deter and adequately withstand Arab attacks. Her territorial integrity was not respected; she did not enjoy secure boundaries, nor were they recognized by neighboring Arab states. In fact, the Arab view of Israel as an unnatural, artificial entity was based on the narrow, zigzag borders that left her strategically vulnerable to enemy aggression, particularly from Syria in the north and Jordan in the east. In Arab eyes Israel was a target too tempting to pass up. In that situation a doctrine of deterrence can hardly be effective — and was not. A doctrine of activist defence became, instead, the de facto Israeli strategy.

The thrust of U.S. policy is to accept both above clauses in principle, suggesting that Israel will abandon all post-'67 territories (a), but will achieve through peace with the Arabs 'secure and recognized boundaries' (b). Thus, the boundaries which did not serve to prevent war and left Israel strategically weakened and exposed will now become — through peace — militarily viable. This veritable slight of hand denies Israel territory, but accords her security. American Ambassador in 1978 for Middle East peace negotiations, Alfred Atherton, Jr., provided the following typical formulation of this U.S. position:

> We understand the very real security con-
> cerns posed for Israel by withdrawal from
> occupied territory. But we also believe
> that without withdrawal, coupled with
> meaningful security arrangements, there
> can be no peace, and without peace... Is-
> rael can have no true security. The goal
> has to be the territorial integrity and sov-
> ereignty of all states in the area.[13]

In spite of an American recognition of Israel's
"very real security concerns" within the '67 lines,
Mideast peace is not achievable, nor will its benefits be available to all including Israel, without
Israel once again coming face to face with those
"very real security concerns" after withdrawal.
The territories are *implicitly* recognized here as
vital to Israeli security; yet their possession is an
Israeli liability as the Arabs refuse peace under
these circumstances. With an ironic and cruel
twist, America calls upon Israel to realize her
'true' interests and to abandon the territorial 'liability' slung around her neck in 1967.

The notion that Israel can have security in the
pre-'67 frontiers ignores the history of twenty
years of conflict and three wars (1948, 1956,
1967). It also ignores the elementary strategic requirements of a tiny state surrounded by power-
fully-armed Arab neighbors. A persistent American refusal to appreciate Israeli security needs,
in territorial terms, leaves the US unprepared to

foresee at times Israeli military activism (in Lebanon) or political entrenchment (in West Bank-
Judea and Samaria). Related to this is an unwillingness to take seriously the Jewish ideological
spirit seeking concrete form in Judea/Samaria,
which Israel conceives to be the core of her historic homeland. From the American viewpoint it
will be preferable to understand this phenomenon, rather than just reject it, in order to better
articulate a viable US policy strategy towards
Israel on this vital issue.

Of paramount importance in the entire Mideast peace puzzle is the "Palestinian Problem"
'in all its aspects.' For America this issue demands a political and territorial solution, even
though it was referred to in 242 as a humanitarian and refugee problem. This US policy departure, *while still calling 242 the sole basis of regional peace-making*, is not only inconsistent but
also a cause of the erosion in Israel's trust in her
American ally. In a substantive manner, Washington policy has not appreciated the Arab
formulation of the term 'Palestinian Problem'
which is, justifiably, the only formulation the Israelis take seriously. The traditional Arab conception conceives the essence of the problem to
be the Jewish presence in Palestine and the denial of Arab sovereignty over the entire country.[14] With this in mind Israel's anxiety about
Palestinian aspirations becomes more compre-
hensible. America's awareness of this can make

for a more effective US approach on this critical problem in general and Arab autonomy in Judea and Samaria in particular.

A last instance of a faulty understanding of Israeli behavior relates to the start of the Egyptian-Israeli political dialogue and negotiations in November 1977. Initially the US administration perceived Sadat's trip to Jerusalem as inconsistent with an overall 'Geneva-style' approach to regional peace. Sadat was not encouraged; by implication, neither was Begin. However, Israel's overwhelmingly positive reception of Sadat and Begin's willingness to abandon the Sinai *in toto* compelled US compliance with the process.

The Americans were clearly surprised that Prime Minister Begin, touted as a hard-liner, was ready to concede all of Sinai — its strategic territory and passes, the oil wells, the airfields, and the Jewish settlements — to Egypt. Three explanations help unravel Begin's forthcoming offer: 1) the sense of Israeli security deriving from the relatively wide expanse of Sinai; 2) the lack of a clear ideological Zionist imperative over Sinai; and 3) the Prime Minister's aspiration to be the Israeli peace-maker, both for national reasons of Israeli welfare and for personal reasons to 'live down' his 'terrorist' past in pre-state days as leader of the *Irgun* against the British mandatory power. Unaware of these motives, US policy makers were confounded (somewhat happily) by

Israel's yield of all Sinai to Egypt. Standing out in the cold, the Americans only then started to warm up to the action. Rigid patterns of thinking and false stereotypes have not disposed US administrations to capture the deeper forces operating on Israeli policy towards the regional conflict. Yet those forces are likely to continue affecting the major positions held by any Israeli government. On security, territorial, and 'Palestinian' questions Israel sees the challenges as central to her capacity for national survival. Here we touch on the third circle calling for a rethinking of American policy on the Middle East.

* * *

The present era we are living through is a turning point in world history. Beyond the colossal military contests and national revolutions in this century, the primary thrust of developments focuses now on the viability of Western civilization itself. For many centuries the Western world incorporated ideas and values from Jewish, Greek, Christian, and other cultural traditions. It formed the basic beliefs of a civilization that included notions of human freedom, personal dignity, the rule of law, and justice according to right and not might. It consolidated an image of man who elevated reason over instinct and communal consciousness over selfish egoism. Peace and cooperation were its ideals in place of violence and discord. Human life had a supreme value and government was an instrument to assure mankind's welfare. It is not an exaggeration to suggest, rather warn, that only if the right decisions are made today will Western society arrive at a better tomorrow. Without the right decisions, there may never be a tomorrow worth living to see.

The American vision is in particular a culmination of the most fundamental principles of Western civilization. The founding fathers of the republic intended the liberated colonies to fulfill the dream of freedom in all forms and to spread that dream to the entire new world. A contemporary political formulation, from the Carter administration's proposed budget for the fiscal year ending September 30, 1981, read as follows:

> U.S. foreign policy seeks a world that is at peace and abides by commonly accepted rules of international law, a world that provides opportunities for people everywhere to meet their basic human needs, and a world where there is respect for human rights and dignity.

This expresses the American hope. The following statement by Paul Johnson, a noted British writer, expresses something closer to the Western reality:

> The principles of objective science and human reason, the notion of the rule of law, the paramountcy of politics over

force, are everywhere undergoing pur-
poseful challenge, and the forces of sav-
agery and violence which constitute this
challenge are becoming steadily bolder,
more numerous and, above all, better
armed.[15]

Only a clear and courageous examination of the
dangers posed against Western civilization will
make the American hope a possible reality rather
than an illusory dream. The dangers are based
on two principal foundations, which will first be
separately noted prior to considering their joint
combined threat.

a) The Soviet Union, in the words of US congressman Jack Kemp, "is the only nation that
poses a comprehensive threat to the political,
cultural, and physical survival of the United States."[16] Driven by an expansionist ideological impulse, and benefitting from the strongest military
machine in the world (maybe in history), the
Russians have the intention and the capacity to
spread their power globally. General Keegan,
former head of US Air Force Intelligence, testified to a Senate committee in 1977 concerning
the Middle East goals of Soviet policy:

...Central among Soviet objectives is the
fomenting of instability, crisis and war
throughout the region. The USSR's principal target is the Persian Gulf, in full

appreciation that NATO's Achilles Heel
is its fuel energy dependency upon the oil-
producing nations of the Middle East.
The Soviets continue to be a principal
backer of every major radical revolution-
ary movement in the Middle East,
whether it be in Iran, Iraq, Lebanon,
Syria, Saudi Arabia, Egypt or Libya.
Among the USSR's objectives... to dis-
place the present feudal Arab leaderships
with radical elements such as has been the
case in Libya, Angola, Somalia and
Ethiopia.[17]

The impact of Russia's military and political
penetration of the Mideast has particular perti-
nence in the economic and ideological fields.

The prosperity of Western civilization — America, Europe, Japan — is, among other factors,
dependent on the flow of oil from Arab-Muslim
countries. Soviet intervention in the critical Persian Gulf zone is made feasible by Russian presence in, or ties with, Afghanistan, Iraq, People's
Democratic Republic of Yemen, Syria, Dhofar
rebels in Oman, PLO terrorists, Libya, Ethiopia,
and Somalia.[18] USSR naval forces in the region
of the Indian Ocean are considerable and growing. In January 1980 Soviet ships stood at the
mouth of the Strait of Hormuz in the Gulf,
through whose narrow waterway pass about 40
percent of Western oil imports. The presence of

100,000 Russian troops in Afghanistan in February 1980 created a real fear that the drive southward was only a matter of time.

The danger to Western interests in the Persian Gulf is most immediately economic. However, a disruption in the flow of oil to the industrial societies of Western Europe, Japan, and America will undermine their social stability and political equilibrium. Both are based on economic prosperity. The repercussions will be deep and far-reaching; communist (Russian-supported) opposition and insurgency will benefit from the ensuing chaos, particularly in Western Europe. The end of liberal societies and democratic governments will be in sight — lined up, in fact, in the sights of the Soviet sharpshooters.

USSR advances in the Middle East spread the communist message there across ever-wider expanses and threaten to eliminate possibilities in that region and beyond for more open societies than Soviet political methods and models usually permit. The world of democratic, liberal life is squeezed further into a corner. Western values and political norms are unable to grow, or even survive, in this kind of environment. America begins to look like an historical anachronism in an era that does not learn its message or carry its dream. Joseph Churba, former senior Middle East intelligence officer in the US Air Force, has formulated the problem in its most elemental form:

> We, as Americans, must not forget that only the West has interests in the Middle East which it must defend. The Soviet Union has only opportunities for destroying these interests and very few independent interests of its own... It should always be remembered that Moscow does not require dominance in the Middle East to maintain and nurture its political and economic system at home. America cannot say the same.[19]

It is vital to make this position known and credible if the American dream is to sustain itself.

b) The Arab world, with its powerful Islamic religious component, has never been significantly touched by the liberal tradition of Western society. An authoritarian stamp characterizes the culture and politics of Arab countries, while Islam itself is conceived as a fundamentalist creed demanding strict observance. The term 'Muslim' means 'to submit' to the sole authority of Muhammad and his religious laws. Recent Islamic resurgence in the Arab world is a conscious return to, and emphasis of, the most fundamental beliefs and orthodox behavior in Islam, and it is accompanied by a narrow xenophobic impetus propelled by uninhibited violence. It is instructive to recall that the attack in November 1979 against the Great Mosque in

Mecca was carried out in the name of Muslim extremism in an Arâb land — Saudi Arabia — whose religious puritanism had never been suspect. Even there the cry for greater Islamic commitment has been heard.

Islam asserts a religious claim for the supremacy of Muslims over non-Muslims in theology and political matters. The term *dhimmi* is employed to define the 'tolerated' scriptural religions of Judaism and Christianity whose peoples can maintain their faith, yet are relegated to an inferior social status compared to the Muslim power. The fate of Jews and Christians under Islam was at times tolerable and satisfactory, while at other times unbearable and dangerous.[20] Political suppression did not however eliminate culture contact. Yet the religious demarcation always remained to guarantee Muslim-Arab superiority over the other, older monotheistic creeds.

This historical background may have something to do with the recent international assertion of Muslim power in religious forms. One thinks initially of the two big mosques constructed in the heart of Western civilization — Washington and London. Or, in a different place with a different context, the Saudi practise of administering lashes to foreign alcoholic drinkers in accordance with the *sharia* law is indicative of a public display of Islam for Muslims and non-Muslims alike.

American policy has for many years hoped to build up an association with the Muslim world based on Christian-Islamic cooperation. In February 1945 President Roosevelt met with King Ibn Saud at Great Bitter Lake in the Suez Canal and consummated, according to one State Department official, a 'moral alliance. . .cemented between Arabs and Islam, and the West and Christianity'.[21] This modern-day Saladin/Richard the Lion-Hearted encounter was grounded, ultimately, in the oil wells of Arabia more than in the ecumenical spirit of summit diplomacy. A recent version of the American approach was expressed by President Carter in an 1979 Christmas remark:

> But I know that all Americans feel very deeply that the relationship between ourselves and the Moslem believers and the world of Islam is one of respect and care and brotherhood and goodwill and love.

Carter's adviser, Zbigniew Brzezinski, has similarly declared that 'there's a great deal of overlap between Christianity and Islam'.[22] This view is certainly inconsistent with the classic Muslim claim for superiority over the Christian *dhimmi*. The alleged common philosophy between the two religions is rooted more in a Western hope than an Eastern reality. Egyptian oppression of Copts, Muslim opposition to Lebanese Maronites, and Iraqi destruction of Orthodox Nestorians are case studies worth American attention.

Terrorism to advance political goals constitutes a violent and more direct Arab threat to the West. The PLO benefitting from Saudi, Libyan, and other Arab assistance, has become the international core of numerous groups — the Red Brigades, IRA, Baader-Meinhof, Carlos' links, etc. — whose consistent targets are the Western world. Enjoying Soviet support and material assistance, PLO terrorism has struck at American diplomats (Khartoum and Beirut), Italian airports, the British legal process, and French order in the streets of Paris. Its violence has violated Western norms of peace and respect for national sovereignty; and the West, bound by inner restraints and confounded by fear of Arab blackmail and sanctions, has capitulated to the lawlessness of PLO terrorism. Perhaps more disturbing is the role of the Western media who explain away this violent phenomenon, apologize for its excesses and also sympathize with its members — who are either 'misguided and unstable' or 'idealistic and well-motivated.' If the PLO is a group of 'freedom-fighters' or 'guerilla forces', then their terrorist barbarity has been condoned and there is no longer any independent Western standard of morality to judge acts against civilization.

The oil weapon against the West, used so powerfully since the 1973 Mideast War, has led to a decay in the fabric of international cooperation. OPEC and OAPEC have unilaterally raised oil prices approximately 1000 per cent from 1973 to 1980. The West has succumbed — due to its economic dependency, political ineffectiveness, and military paralysis. Some of America's alleged close Arab friends, like the Saudis, have also been part of this oil campaign and even led the embargo against the United States in 1973-74.

The appeasement of Arab oil warfare has gone hand in hand with capitulating to Arab military aggression. One basic point should suffice: in spite of a history of Arab attacks against Israel designed to weaken and destroy her, the West has consistently supported every Arab claim since 1948 to recover territory lost in its aggressive efforts against Israel. Thereby, the Arabs pay no price for aggression and Western standards of moral responsibility and legal equity are trampled on in the Western stampede to win favor in the eyes of the Sixth Superpower: the Arab-Muslim world.

The West may certainly not be justified in drawing the moral distinctions between itself and the Arab world with the excessive *hubris* of one Nikephoros Phokas who conquered Tarsus in 965.[23] However, it may still learn from him that there is a legitimate place to differentiate, at least in relativist terms, the striving for civilizational norms from their utter rejection by the other side.

The twin threats to Western society from Soviet Russia and Arab Islam have joined forces on a number of occasions. Their alliance, it should be noted, rests on three fundamental identities that make external cooperation a natural consequence. From an internal perspective they share the following characteristics:

1) both societies are organized by *totalitarian regimes* that limit individual liberties and political freedom and deify the State that is led by a small elite group;

2) both societies are highly *militaristic* emphasizing the role of the army in national life and policy-making; and

3) both societies are motivated by *ideological* radicalism that seeks to upset the status quo and institute wide-ranging changes in regional and global power relations.

These features in Soviet Russia and Arab Islam make of both societies the locus of a clear vision of ultimate national goals, formulated in ideological terms, and the core of concentrated policy planning to realize such goals, formulated in strategic terms. Ray Cline, former Deputy Director for Intelligence at the CIA and presently Executive Director of the Center for Strategic and International Studies at Georgetown University, has faulted America for its lack of strategic direction, unable to know who its enemies are and what is worth fighting for, without policy rigor and coherence.[24] The Russians and the Arabs, however, know where they want to go and how to go about getting there.

Links between the USSR and the Arab world began to tighten in the 1950's when Russian weapons began arming Arab forces. Relations developed into diplomatic cooperation in the 1960's and led to treaties in the 1970's between such states as Egypt, Syria, Iraq, and Southern Yemen with the Soviet Union. These formal ties, while indicative of growing coordination of purposes, must not lead us to lose sight of the more critical and practical collusion carried out in a number of instances to the detriment of Western interests. Here is a list of cases of Russian-Arab strategic cooperation:

* The 1973 war was a combined Soviet-Arab planning scheme against Israel and its American ally. In May 1972 Brezhnev and Nixon signed the "Basic Principles of Relations between the USSR and the USA". This document stipulated that both countries would 'make every effort to remove the threat of war' and that they both 'attach major importance to preventing the development of situations capable of causing a dangerous exacerbation of their relations'. They promised to 'always exercise restraint in their mutual relations'. Yet there is evidence that already at that time the Russians were helping Sadat plan the '73 war, thereby flouting the '72

document in America's face.[25] The continual supply of USSR arms to Egypt (even after the 'expulsion' of Soviet personnel in July 1972), the adherence of Arab warfare to Soviet military doctrine, the evacuation of Soviet people from Egypt a few days prior to the outbreak of war, and the immediate inauguration of a massive airlift — all indicated the strategic role of the Russians in planning and executing the Arab war.[26] The Kremlin wanted, as a consequence of the end of the political deadlock in the region, to have Israel pushed away from the Suez Canal and the waterway opened. It rebegan operations in June 1975 and no naval force has more benefited than that of the Soviet Union, now easily penetrating the Indian Ocean. It was, again according to Soviet and Arab strategy, the Americans who would push Israel away from the Canal zone.

* The 1973-74 Arab oil embargo was encouraged, if not instigated, by Russia's effort to divide NATO and weaken Western strength economically, politically, and militarily. This USSR-Arab collusion impaired US military readiness and mobility as Arab oil-producers prevented American forces from acquiring fuel from refineries in those countries which buy crude oil from the Arabs — such as Singapore and Spain. Under pressure from Arab oil embargo threats, a number of European allies — such as Italy — refused the U.S. landing rights for Air Force

planes transporting military equipment to the be-
leaguered Israeli army in the beginning of the
October War. The overall economic benefits
from the OPEC embargo and price-rise benefited
Arab producers as well as the Soviet Union, itself
an oil exporting nation. Thus, in a variety of
ways the Atlantic Alliance was undermined
based on the successful strategic and economic
coordination of interests by the Russians and the
Arabs.

* Operational cooperation between Russians
and Arabs is strongly felt in the area of PLO
terrorism. KGB officers have trained PLO fighters in the Soviet military academies, this admit-
ted to by PLO UN observer, Zehdi Terzi, in a
New York interview in September 1979. In Iran,
once considered "an important friend [of Amer-
ica] in a critical and unstable part of the world"
by a Senate delegation report from June 1977, [27]
Soviet and PLO forces combined to covertly
overthrow the Shah's regime. Iranian terrorists
were in fact trained by Russian personnel in Palestinian Arab camps. Following the accession of
Khomeini to power, Arafat paid him a special
visit. Their broad smiles and many kisses were a
symbolic gesture to the combined Arab/Muslim-
Soviet victory and the American-Israeli loss.
Once again, Western strategic and oil interests
suffered a grave defeat.

* The attack against the Great Mosque of
Mecca in 1979 enjoyed the vital support of Rus-

sian and PLO forces. Southern Yemen, a Soviet satellite, supplied weapons to the religious zealots, as did Habash's Popular Front for the Liberation of Palestine (PFLP). Saudi prince Fahd linked the Russians to the attack against the holiest shrine in Islam when he noted the Soviet-made weapons used by the attackers.[28] Writing in *Newsweek*, Arnaud de Borchgrave commented that European intelligence services cannot believe that the plot in Saudi Arabia was not known to the KGB.[29] In collaboration with radical Arab elements, Soviet destabilization policies in the Middle East have been instrumental in undermining American-defined national interests.

* A last example of policy identity between the Soviet Union and the Arab world touches upon their diplomatic strategy of détente. The Russian conception of reconciliation with capitalist America does not eliminate continued forms of struggle that, at times, avoid warfare and dangerous conflicts. But conflict as such goes on primarily through economic, ideological, and diplomatic avenues. As noted earlier, 'peaceful coexistence' does not mean the end of the communist struggle for global dominance over America. This model of conflict was then adopted and practised by Anwar Sadat since the '73 war. Its basic proposition is: a settlement with Israel does not imply renunciation of the Arab goal against Zionism. An articulate Egyptian presentation of this strat-

egy was written by Muhammed Sid Ahmed in his book *When The Guns Fall Silent* published in 1975. He called upon the Arab world to cultivate détente with Israel (based on the Soviet-American model) to weaken the enemy and bring about its ultimate destruction through 'peaceful coexistence'. Much of Sadat's post-'73 strategy, in particular the 1978 Camp David Peace, is consistent with the fundamentals of Soviet-style détente. A show of diplomatic moderacy is tactical and the long-range political goal continues to guide the strategic conception. This approach seems to explain what the Soviet policy towards the United States and what the Arab policy towards Israel is really concerned with. Henry Kissinger has perceptively analyzed the Western habit of concessions in negotiations and the deep-seated belief in the solvability of all conflicts.[30] This posture ill-prepares America and Israel to cope with the Soviet and Arab notion of détente as just an alternative form of interstate conflict, or with their commitment to war and peace as merely successive phases of an ongoing struggle.

The Soviet-Arab linkage is solidly based on a variety of shared political principles and strategic practises. It is further grounded in a common historical opposition to the Western role in the Third World, which the Arabs personally experienced and the Russians ideologically rejected. The profound Arab antipathy to Western influence in the Middle East was, in earlier years, a natural ally of Soviet efforts to oust the West from the region. Ever since, and even before, the denunciation of *Zionism and Imperialism* has gone hand in hand. The Arabs opposed Western aid to Israel and the Russians opposed Western penetration of an area considered vital to them in global terms. The diplomatic linkage of 'Zionism and Imperialism' — against Israel and America — has made of the latter two the common object of a persistent propaganda attack.

Yet, this 'negative' foundation for a US-Israel linkage is certainly not critical when compared with the positive identity of principles and purposes that bind the two Western societies in a common civilizational bond. America, globally, is the last bastion that 'safekeeps hope for liberty amongst men', in the words of President Lincoln. Today, that majestic historic task is so crucial if mankind hopes to maintain the flame of freedom burning. Israel, in the Middle East, is the only country committed to the values of individual freedom and political democracy. The American-Israeli linkage is natural and necessary to face the Soviet-Arab onslaught on the very fabric of Western civilization.

Traditional American policy in the Mideast has been closely allied to Arab power, meaning Saudi Arabia and Egypt primarily. This orientation closely approximates England's strategy, America's Western predecessor in the region, when in earlier decades the British imperium cultivated friendly relations with a number of leading Arab personalities and states at the expense of its commitment to the Zionist revival. This historical analogy of reliance on the Arabs to achieve basic Western interests is not a very encouraging one indeed. With the help of a Soviet strategy of 'divide and rule' (evict the British from Egypt with the help of the United States and then establish a Russian presence there), the Arabs have successfully preserved their national independence and have often acted in ways harmful to the Western powers.

This has not, nevertheless, significantly altered the American Establishment policy paradigm of a close relationship with the Arabs to achieve US interests. Whether this is appropriate policy or ignoble appeasement is not the immediate question, though a judgment on this point is surely worth considering. The initial issue is to describe how America has conceived her interests in the Middle East and the optimal approach towards their fulfillment. It will be vital to examine whether US policy has been able to cultivate wise political statesmanship in the service of the principles of Western civilization. And we must never lose sight of what is at stake in this era of history, as we inquire into America's Middle East policy.

Stripped of their specious justifications about past Western exploitation and the intolerable affront to Arab susceptibilities afforded by the existence of Israel, the actions of the Arabs and the Persians before, during and since 1973, if placed in their historical, religious, racial and cultural setting, amount to nothing less than a bold attempt to lay the Christian West under tribute to the Muslim East.

> J.B. Kelly,
> *Arabia, The Gulf and the West.*

Alcibiades: ... there's one thing I've never felt with anybody else — not the kind of thing you'd expect to find in me, either — and that is a sense of shame. Socrates is the only man in the world that can make me feel ashamed. Because there's no getting away from it, I know I ought to do the things he tells me to, and yet the moment I'm out of his sight I don't care what I do to keep in with the mob.

> Plato,
> *Symposium,* 216b

CHAPTER 2:

COMPETING CONCEPTIONS OF THE U.S. NATIONAL INTEREST

The background and basis to this analysis of American policy in the Middle East will draw upon three documents composed in the 1970's dealing with this question. Two of them have much in common: *Toward Peace in the Middle East*, 1975, by the Brookings Institution,[1] and *Oil and Turmoil: Western Choices in the Middle East*, 1979, by the Atlantic Council.[2] Both studies were prepared by personalities who have been close to Washington policy-making circles, connected with the State Department and the National Security Council. The names of Brzezinski, Kerr, Scowcroft, Campbell, and others having close links with the Establishment approach in American thinking towards the Mideast appear on the lists of participants. Although neither document represented *official* American thinking, the membership of both study groups suggests a semi-official linkage at least.

There is, however, a more substantial reason to consider the Brookings and Atlantic Council papers in the context of American national conceptions regarding the Middle East. Their policy content and practical recommendations closely approximate official Establishment thinking, and this is valid for past administrations and for the present Reagan administration as well. This makes of their work much more than an academic exercise. Both, for example, call for a complete Israeli withdrawal from all territories taken in the 1967 war; this position has been official American policy since 1969 with the appearance of the Rogers proposals.

More significant yet is the political trend apparent in comparing the substance of both documents separated by four, rather full, years. Three points of difference, in substance, emphasis, and nuance, indicate a deeper association between American and Arab thinking. The Atlantic Council report in particular reflects the more 'balanced', meaning more 'Arab', orientation in Washington diplomatic directions towards the end of the '70's. Note the following points:

1) The Brookings document defined "the security, independence, and well-being of Israel" as an American interest. The Atlantic Council report noted only that the U.S. is committed to

Israel's "independence and security", but did not see her as an American interest as such. (Chapter 3 discusses in detail the distinction between Israel as a U.S. 'interest' or Israel as worthy of an American 'commitment'.) By 1979 Israel is even impugned as seeking her security through methods of 'war and terrorism'.[3]

2) The Brookings document advocates "the right of the Palestinians to self-determination in one form or another" without, however, determining the exact political concretization or deciding on the national leadership of this people. The Atlantic Council report makes clear its view that the 'question of Arab Palestinians... remains at the heart of the Arab-Israeli conflict'.[4] This formulation approximates official thinking as articulated by Assistant Secretary of State Saunders before Congress on November 12, 1975. In addition, the report calls on America to 'maintain informal contact with the PLO'. In contrast the Brookings document noted that the PLO claim to represent Arabs in the territories 'is not unchallenged'. The lack of reciprocal Israel-PLO recognition seemed to disqualify a role for the PLO in the opinion of the document.[5] The Council's support for informal contacts with the PLO, written in 1979, coincided with the Young-Terzi meeting in New York when the U.S. Ambassador to the United Nations conferred with the PLO spokesman who enjoys Observer Status at the international body.

3) The Brookings document notes the U.S. interest "in an unimpeded flow of Middle Eastern oil to itself and to its European and Japanese allies." This interest appears as one among a number of American interests and is listed third in order of importance. In the Atlantic Council presentation oil is at the top of the list: its unrivalled centrality is expressed in the following terms by Kenneth Rush, Chairman of the Atlantic Council in the United States, in his Foreword to the report:

> We in the Western World must not make the vital mistake of considering OPEC as the arch enemy that has brought on all our problems by precipitately raising oil prices, stimulating the inflationary trend, and throwing our economies out of order. Actually the modern industrial nations and the oil producing countries have much in common... Cooperation rather than conflict must be the keynote in our relations with the OPEC countries.

Rush minimizes the economic damages caused by spiralling OPEC prices and acquits its mainly Arab-Muslim members of any moral or political responsibility for their use of the oil weapon against the West. Oil is not only a Western interest. It has become a by-word for appeasement, its producers and manipulators — not enemies — but friends.

The differences in the perception of Israel, the Palestinian issue and oil from the Brookings document to the Atlantic Council report — from 1975 to 1979 — reflect a growing identification between American, European, and Arab views and policies regarding the Mideast conflict. This is the period of President Carter's call for a 'Palestinian homeland' (1977) and America's 'full partnership' role with Egypt and against Israel to achieve a comprehensive settlement following the Camp David Accords of 1978.

These developments are sufficient to indicate that the dominant U.S. conception of its national interest in the Mideast is primarily based on a pro-Arab political outlook. Clearly there are historical foundations for this trend that suggest, not only its novelty, but also its rootedness in American thinking. Philip Baram's study of the State Department highlights three components of U.S. Mideastern policy that give the trend of the '70s a historical context. He notes:

1) the primacy of economic considerations in State political priorities that tilted the balance in favor of Arab oil and trade benefits in the American interest;

2) the existence of anti-Semitism among many department officials which distorted their objectivity and colored their opposition to Zionism and Israel's establishment; and

3) the support for national self-determination of small peoples, sometimes theoretical and not

practised, but which can, due to conceptual routine or historical consistency, account for present advocacy of Palestinian national rights against Israel.[6]

To the degree these background factors are operative in American official thinking today, then one must see the pro-Arab bias not as a radical distortion of U.S. policy but as a consistent feature of it. The above economic goals, racial prejudices, and political notions will undoubtedly continue to guide policy so long as they are seen to bring benefits to America. Only a realization of the grave disadvantages incurred from this approach, and the considerations that underly it, could bring about a reassessment of its political logic.

A third document on America's Mideast policy is the brief statement composed to warn against current trends that endanger world peace and U.S. security, written in 1978 and signed by over 170 retired admirals and generals.[7] It is worth noting that it is many of these people who later played a major role in the Presidential campaign to elect Reagan and who hoped that his victory would bring about an improvement of American-Israeli ties. Sent as a letter to President Carter, the fear of growing Soviet power sets the tone for the generals' deep anxieties. USSR penetration of the Mideast threatens the flow of oil to the West, this explicated prior to the Shah's fall and the Soviet aggression against

Afghanistan. Events in 1979-80 seemed definitely to confirm the document's realistic view of world and regional trends that threaten American welfare and security.

Unlike the dominant Establishment view in the United States, Israel and not the Arabs is considered America's primary Middle Eastern support and ally. Of critical significance is Israel's military capacity to assist in the protection of Western interests, both strategic and oil, in what is a volatile region of the world. This political conception specifically calls upon the President to adhere to America's mission to defend freedom around the globe and to fulfill that task in association with her allies and friends, specifically Western Europe, Japan, and Israel. No Arab state is mentioned among the fighters for freedom against the Soviet threat.

The letter of the military élite did not represent the national vision or set of priorities dominating Washington policy-making. It no doubt is supported by certain elements whose voice is not sufficiently heard or not authoritatively recognized.[8] In itself, nevertheless, the document points to an alternative American course of action where Western interests are vital and vulnerable. An American debate on Mideast policy should examine all possible options in an effort to gain maximum information, intellectual breadth, and policy maneuverability. This now established, set against the backdrop of three policy reports —Brookings, Atlantic Council, and the Generals' Letter — the major conception and counter-conception of U.S. political thinking will be detailed. This review of the thinking and intentions underlying American policy will entail as well an examination of the results and consequences in practise.

Elements in the National Interest

Three basic problems preoccupy American thinking on the Middle East: the Arab-Israeli conflict and the need to eliminate regional tension and create a binding Mideast peace; Soviet penetration of the region and the imperative of U.S. security concerns against Russian forces; and reliance on oil imports from Arab-Muslim countries that have embargoed the West, raised prices astronomically in the 1970's and the need to guarantee a steady flow of this strategic resource at reasonable costs during times of peace and times of tension and war.

This triple American headache is not considered a haphazard list of national ills, but rather a causally-linked set of problems whose overall source and solution derive from a single origin. The dominant conception identifies the source of the Soviet threat to American interests and the oil danger to Western stability as a consequence of the unresolved Arab-Israeli conflict. To solve that conflict is, according to this view, the necessary precondition to handle, or eliminate, the

Soviet threat and to neutralize the use of the oil weapon by the Arabs. As a result, the U.S. priority becomes Middle East peace-making as a step to tackling the other two outstanding problems. The advantage of examining American interests in this manner lies in its realistic grounding as an approach to U.S. policy-making. This does not guarantee, however, that the choice of priorities is necessarily 'realistic'. It only suggests that it should be, and if it is not, then there is room to consider an alternative — and more realistic — approach.

(1) The Arab-Israeli Conflict

The dominant American conception closely identifies the Middle East as a region with the Arab-Israeli conflict to the degree that the latter problem is nearly coterminous with what is significant within the Mideast itself. If this was an accurate judgment, then it logically follows that other regional problems, with no independent vitality of their own, are merely offshoots of the unresolved Arab-Israeli conflict. From this it is inferred that a resolution of the intractable conflict will remove the last obstacle to successfully coping with the Soviet threat and to a guaranteed, uninterrupted flow of oil from Arab producing countries.

The Brookings paper is explicit on this linkage: "Rising tensions in the Middle East... might well lead to another Arab-Israeli war and even provoke a major confrontation between the United States and the Soviet Union, substantially elevating East-West tension and threatening the recent manysided effort toward greater international stability."[9] The regional conflict is identified as a global threat and even, it is hinted, a possible catalyst to a Third World War between the superpowers. The Atlantic Council report similarly considers the Arab-Israeli conflict 'a threat to world peace' demanding, therefore, a quick settlement. America's ability to confront the Soviet threat to the Mideast depends, in part, on improving the political and economic position of the U.S. with its allies who are mainly Arab-Muslim states. This approach is based, therefore, on a settlement of the Arab-Israeli conflict which will satisfy Arab aspirations that will bring them, as a consequence, closer to the American camp in the region. Once it has been established, in the language of the Atlantic Council, that the "Arab-Israeli conflict remains central to the evolution of the entire Middle East and to American and Western interests there,"[10] then the proposed settlement will be an immediate political imperative pursued with great urgency. Like the Americans, the Arabs too believe in the necessity of a rapid resolution of the conflict. Israel, however, has been wary of rapid momentum that will strip her of strategic well-being prior to the time when the stability and safety promised by the process of real peace-making become an authentic part of Israeli-Arab relations.

The solution to the conflict is needed, not only to avoid superpower confrontation, but to assure the continued flow of oil to the West. Recognizing the West's dependence on imported oil, the Brookings report declares: "In the event of another Arab-Israeli war, or even a serious crisis short of war, Arab oil shipments to those markets might be disrupted."[11] No doubt the Arab embargo during the 1973 war is uppermost in the minds of the authors here. The Atlantic Council document is based on an implicit assumption, nowhere made explicit but nonetheless instrumental to the thrust of its argument, that only a resolution of the conflict and developing closer US ties with the Arabs can assure a safe, unimpeded flow of oil. In fact, the great emphasis on the oil issue and the pro-Arab (and pro-PLO) slant are proof of this point.

The conception outlined here, which bases the realization of US interests upon the solution of the Arab-Israeli conflict, did not begin in the 1970's. John Badeau, a former American Ambassador to Egypt, noted the dependence of oil supplies upon the termination of the regional rivalry in his pro-Arab study called *The American Approach to the Arab World* published in 1968.[12] Since then, with the worsening oil situation and a growing Western tendency to accede to Arab

CHAPTER 2 · 63

claims against Israel, this view is heard more often.

Here are examples from 1979 in the words of two major American political figures. First from George Ball:

> Since the rise of OPEC as a major factor in world affairs, and particularly since the Western nations' new awareness of their dependence on the policies and actions of the Arab oil-producing states, America's interests have become vitally and directly involved in a speedy settlement of the Arab-Israeli conflict. Already, the splitting of the Arab world by Camp David has created tensions and complications in our relations, not merely with Saudi Arabia but with the other oil-producing states as well...[13]

Ball conceives of the oil problem dependent on satisfying Arab demands in the context of their conflict with Israel. Arab discontent with Camp David, as no other Arab state fully supported Egypt's agreement to the peace treaty with Israel, has according to Ball worsened the likelihood of a smooth supply of oil to the West. John Connally expresses a similar outlook to that of Ball using more dramatic and direct language:

> The oil of the Middle East is and will continue to be the lifeblood of Western

civilization for decades to come! The continued flow of oil from that region is and will continue to be critical to the realization of the aspirations of the millions who live in the developing world. So long as those tensions go unabated, so long as the threat of war remains, there hovers over our nation and all the nations of the West, the awful specter of economic upheaval, social disruption and political chaos... we must secure a clear understanding from Saudi Arabia and other moderate oil-producing nations in the region that a just and comprehensive peace settlement means a return to stable oil prices in real terms. The Arabs must, in short, forsake the oil weapon in return for Israel's withdrawal from the occupied territories.

... The last Middle East war in 1973 edged us forward to confrontation with the Soviet Union. It is not an overstatement to say that another conflict could lead to World War III.[14]

An air of desperation is pushing Connally to expedite a quick peace solution upon which, so he believes, the welfare of the Western world depends. An air of naiveté underlies his belief that America can compel the proud and independent Arab states to commit themselves to supply oil to the West in a controlled and stable manner.

The conception presented in the 1970's contains a new element in the attempt to resolve the Arab-Israeli conflict. Now the Palestinian problem becomes 'the heart', or core, of the entire political deadlock, making the solution of that particular issue the predominant focus of attention. In his speech before the UN General Assembly on September 24, 1979 Secretary of State Vance declared 'that an ultimate settlement must address the legitimate rights of the Palestinian people'. The latter phrase — 'the legitimate rights of the Palestinian people' — was already part of the Camp David Accords on Arab autonomy completed in September 1978. At around that time Zbigniew Brzezinski told the World Jewish Congress in New York that Israel, beyond concern for her security requirements, "bears a responsibility to reach out to the Palestinians in new and creative ways." American policy-making, following the Arab lead, became more and more convinced that only a most forthcoming gesture to the Palestinians would persuade them to join the peace process begun by Israel and Egypt. Without assuring Palestinian involvement it was feared that the tender tree of peace planted at Camp David would be uprooted in an abrupt and violent fashion. This would endanger not only the Israeli-Egyptian treaty, but Middle East stability which could undermine Western interests in oil supply and Soviet containment. *The St. Paul Dispatch* of January 2, 1980 warned that 'if the Palestinian problem is not solved, it can only continue to poison U.S.-Arab relations and make the task of protecting our vital national interests in the Middle East perilously — and unnecessarily — difficult'.

This political conception, based on a consistent inner logic of its own, has decided that the global complex of problems facing America in the Middle East can be reduced to one single issue. This assumes that the Arab use of the oil weapon, for example, is a response to grave dissatisfaction over the absence of full Palestinian rights (self-determination, sovereignty, and refugee-return) that a resolution of the Arab-Israeli conflict would assure. One of the hardest tasks of social science, and its most basic purpose, is to locate a causal link between two variables, one independent and the other dependent. It is not uncommon for people to fall victim to what is called 'the fallacy of false cause' when offering an incorrect reason to explain a certain phenomenon. It happens that this error arises out of a "self-fulfilling prophecy" whereby merely saying an event will happen helps make it happen.[15] Fearing an Arab use of the oil weapon, America may at times act in a way that assures its usage in order, from the Arab viewpoint, that America keep believing in the likelihood of its threat against the West. This process can only assist the

Arabs in appreciating their leverage over America once America itself has *already* come to believe in it. The practise of specifying the Palestinian root to the Mideast conflict and, by consequence, the Achilles' Heel of Western interests is an attempt at clarification. It may, however, be an exercise in obfuscation and self-delusion. This unfortunate point has apparently become as characteristic of the Reagan administration as it was of its predecessor, as lucidly argued by Professor Robert Tucker in his article, "The Middle East: Carterism Without Carter?" that appeared in the September 1981 issue of *Commentary* magazine.

The US recognition of Palestinian rights has led, ever so slowly yet persistently, to an acceptance of the PLO's role. George Ball and John Connally have both endorsed a need for the American Administration to talk with the PLO now and it may only be a matter of time before Washington does so openly and officially. While representing the U.S. at the funeral of Anwar Sadat in Cairo in October 1981, two former American Presidents, Gerald Ford and Jimmy Carter, voiced their support for Washington starting a dialogue with the PLO, and this in total contravention of the American commitment given to Israel in 1975 not to do so.

After a cease-fire was established in July on the Lebanese border, following Israeli-PLO armed hostilities, there was an attempt to interpret that as an indirect American (and Israeli) readiness to deal with the PLO. In terms of America's Atlantic allies, the European Council issued a statement on June 29, 1977 affirming its belief that the Mideast conflict could not be solved unless the "legitimate right of the Palestinian people to give effective expression to its national identity is translated into fact, which would take into account the need for a homeland for the Palestinian people."[16]

However, the European Community of the Ten has in the Venice Declaration of 1980 formally recognized the PLO and certain European politicians like Brandt, Kreisky, Cheysson and Carrington have already sat in conversation with Arafat. While the Europeans have brought the PLO to center stage the Americans, perhaps agitated and tempted to do likewise, have so far kept them in the wings.

There is a growing belief that the PLO is divided between moderates and extremists and that it is possible, and certainly practical, to cultivate the moderate Arafat-led wing that will eventually bring the terrorist movement to the negotiating table. The grounds for this distinction are, and have been, totally invalid: *all PLO groups* agree that the long-term goal is and must be Israel's complete destruction.[17] That is hardly a 'moderate' position by any standard. This notion of moderacy is a general perspective regarding Arab regimes throughout the region, making it an advisable American tactic to support those kinds of countries in any diplomatic departure. Former Assistant Secretary of State Harold Saunders, in a testimony before the House Sub-committee on Europe and the Middle East on June 12, 1978, noted that an Israeli-Arab peace settlement 'would strengthen moderate govern-ments in the region and enhance U.S. global in-terests'. Thus, America's Mideast policy seeks to keep moderate (i.e., anti-Soviet) regimes in the US political orbit and the way to do that is to satisfy their claims against Israel. Consistent with this conception is to assure PLO participa-tion sooner or later if that seems to be the only method to preserve the peace, or create it, and maintain America's standing in the Arab world. On all of this, therefore, hinges the realization of the most vital Western interests.

For the moment, the counter-thesis to the dominant Establishment foreign policy concep-tion will limit itself, by and large, to the problem of the Arab-Israeli conflict. Later sections will take up the Soviet and oil issues in more detail, accompanied by the critique of the opposing conception. The present counter-thesis will focus on responding to the major assumptions of the dominant view in Washington, summarized as follows:

Assumption 1: The Arab-Israeli conflict is co-terminous with the Middle East.

The Generals' Letter of 1978 does not mention
the conflict at all in addressing itself to the
dangers facing America in the Mideast. The Soviet threat, and with it the oil threat, undermine
the welfare of the Free World *not* due to the
persistence of the Arab-Israeli conflict but based
on America's weakness in coping with global
challenges based in the region. Overcoming the
melancholy of defeatism, particularly after Vietnam, is the immediate American imperative
rather than seeking salvation in Arab goodwill.
It is naive to assume that the manifold problems
of the United States in the Middle East would be
resolved by just terminating the Arab-Israeli
conflict. The only credible solution will be when
America itself, through her own resources and
actions, directly tackles the dangers themselves.

William Quandt, former Director of Middle
East Affairs in the National Security Council,
has provided a penetrating analysis of the unjus-
tified stress on the conflict in perceptions on the
region. In an address at Chatham House in London in June 1979, interestingly when no longer
serving in an official capacity, he said:

> I think the net effect of these three or four
> changes, the change in Iran, the oil revo-
> lution, the Egypt-Israel treaty, and the
> complexities of rapid socio-economic
> modernization particularly in the oil-rich
> countries, has been to create new forms

of instability, threats to established or-
ders and to make the Arab-Israeli conflict
itself perhaps less central to the political
dynamics of the region and to make
energy politics, oil, and the geographical
region around the Persian Gulf more critical and essential.[18]

Quandt offers a perceptive look at the variety of
disturbances that are internal to the political
fabric of Mideast life in the Arab world. He rejects the singular diplomatic emphasis focused
on the Arab-Israeli arena, while avoiding or un-
derestimating developments in the Persian Gulf
and the Arabian Peninsula. In the latter areas, he
warns, America's interests 'will not simply take
care of themselves' nor will they be assured
through an Israeli-Arab peace even if attained.

Much of Carter's Middle East efforts had in
fact been dedicated to a resolution of the conflict
or at least its containment. His administration
had mediated in the Israeli-Egyptian negotiations; he held a summit at Camp David in 1978
convened for over a full week of intense meet-
ings; and since was very preoccupied with bring-
ing the talks on Autonomy to a successful conclusion, that included summit talks in Washington with Sadat and Begin in April 1980. His
administration labored over the American hostages held in Iran since late 1979, but this preoccupation has little to do with America's funda-

mental problems in the Persian Gulf zone. This imbalance in efforts and time has prevented a national apportioning of US diplomacy to the challenges in the Middle East.

Recognition of Soviet maneuvers in the region is a critical element in Quandt's conception of US problems there. The Russians are now established in strategic positions bordering on Saudi Arabia (from Southern Yemen) and Iran (from Afghanistan). This makes a Soviet thrust to the sources of Western energy supplies a very conceivable military and political possibility. The Generals' Letter, as well as Quandt, views the denial of oil to the West as one of the USSR's imperial objectives. For now all of this is sufficient to appreciate the soundness of the counter-thesis that rejects the notion of the Arab-Israeli conflict as the only issue legitimately demanding the concern of the United States today. The alternative conception sees this as blind ignorance of the complex nature of what the Middle East is really about.

Assumption 2: The Palestinian problem is the core of the Arab-Israeli conflict.

As the generals' Letter does not even refer specifically to the Arab-Israeli conflict, it follows that it completely bypasses the Palestinian problem. Their global perspective does not bother with local details. Yet those who do consider the conflict itself do not all believe that, in this context, the Palestinian issue is central. It will do well to remember that hardly anyone ever goes to the trouble of providing a clear definition of what the "Palestinian problem" is, and few ever requested President Sadat to explicate in detail the exact parameters of the issue as he saw it.

For the Arabs the Palestinian problem is very simple. On March 17, 1968 the "Voice of the Arabs" (Radio Cairo) explained: "The real Palestine problem is the existence of Israel in Palestine. As long as a Zionist existence remains even in a tiny part of it — that will mean occupation." Here the Palestine problem does not refer to the West Bank and Gaza Strip taken by Israel in 1967, but to Israel itself as established in 1948! If this is the core issue that the dominant conception seeks to resolve, then the American-Arab linkage is deadlier than ever imagined.

The Arab-Israeli conflict has involved a number of Arab states, like Syria and Egypt, whose territory was never threatened by Israel but who, during their aggressive campaigns, lost land to Israel. This territorial issue, regarding the Golan Heights for example, has little to do with the Palestinian question. The Syrians, in 1967 and 1973, had much more to do with the creation of border tension and regional warfare than did the Palestinians in those days. To overemphasize the Palestinian issue blinds one to the deep gaps still separating Israel from the Arab states themselves.

Based on the above two points — the true dimensions of the 'Palestinian problem' and general regional hostility to the Jewish state — it must be considered that the real core of the Arab-Israeli conflict is the Arab intention to eliminate Israel from the Middle East. This is the considered judgment of General Keegan, noted earlier and one of the signators of the Letter of 170, when he declared before a Senate subcommittee in 1977 'that the Arab leaders remain committed to the ultimate destruction of the Israeli state'. Consistent with this approach is the recent statement by Professor Elie Kedourie who said: "It is by no means obvious that 'the Palestinian dimension' is the 'heart' of the Arab-Israeli conflict; it could, on the contrary, be argued that it is the least important part of it."[19] If so, what is the most important part of the conflict? It would follow that the Arab rejection of the independent and viable Jewish state of Israel in its homeland remains the heart and core of the conflict. The Palestinian problem turns out to be semantic hogwash or, if you like, diplomatic deception to hide true Arab aspirations and concerns while flouting Madison Avenue's most tantilizing PR slogan in this century — 'the Palestinian problem'. Admittedly, in order to expose the false argument of a Palestinian core to the Arab-Israeli conflict, it would be necessary to review the history of the Jewish-Arab conflict in Palestine, the development of the regional rivalry, the background of Arab settlement in the Land of Israel, and the degree of a distinctive national identity and collective cohesion among Palestinian Arabs. This is not possible in our context, but having outlined the most fundamental weaknesses of the Arab-American claim is sufficient to raise grave doubts as to its authenticity.

A last point on this question: if Arab states, like Egypt until now, declare the Palestinian issue to be the core of the conflict, this signifies that the Arabs have *chosen* to make it the core of the conflict. This policy decision is not a political necessity based on historical determinism; it is a freely-taken decision based on Arab views concerning the conflict itself. Therefore, the Palestinian problem becomes the core of the conflict for them because they have decided *to make it* the core of the conflict. It did not have to be this way, but it is this way because they have made it so. Their support for this issue is the critical factor and not the factor itself, which derives its force only because the Arab states have adopted it as part of their own national concerns. It follows from this that the real core of the conflict is Arab opposition to Israel expressed through their support for the Palestinian claim against Israel.

Assumption 3: The PLO may need to be part of regional peace-making to achieve a settlement and strengthen US interests.

The positive disposition to a PLO role in Mideast peace-making is rejected by the alternative conception as short-sighted and impractical. While Saunders tried to squeeze out moderate interpretations from PLO pronouncements in mid-1979 and claimed that the Palestinian movement wants 'to keep its options open' on the Camp David negotiations,[20] the Russian-PLO alliance grew stronger all the time. The patronizing and unrealistic attempt to entice a fundamental change in PLO ideology and goals is a totally lame effort. It fortifies a Soviet proxy whose threat to US interests would prove even more catastrophical if the American attempt at helping the PLO worked. As it is now Palestinian elements already pose a grave threat to US interests, oil and other, in Saudi Arabia where their role in the petroleum industry and opposition to a conservative feudal regime make them a potential 'fifth column' on a permanent basis. The PLO has in fact warned Saudi Arabia of the vulnerability of its oil fields, and the $40 million allocated annually to PLO coffers are designed to offset that precarious vulnerability as much as is possible. Close to the new Iranian regime, the PLO sits alongside the heart of the West's oil reservoir in the Persian Gulf and Saudi Arabia.[21] The Saudi Minister of Petroleum, Sheikh Yamani, has already cautioned that Palestinian frustration over unfulfilled political expectations might lead PLO forces to blow up an oil tanker headed for the West as it passes through the narrow Strait of Hormuz in the gulf. Remember: a tanker passes through every eleven minutes.

The likelihood of a pro-Soviet, radical, anti-Western PLO turning into America's best friend seems like a farfetched political gamble indeed. Even should the US administration succeed to scathe some territory off Israel for a Palestinian 'homeland', the more likely development is the permanent estrangement of the PLO from the West. Its political character, religious roots, and violent methods make it inimical to Western values and interests. Moreover, the Soviet connection will not easily be loosened. Russian money, guns, and propaganda have been heavily invested in assuring that the voice of the Kremlin will beam out over Palestinian political airwaves. A first-stage PLO state in Judea/Samaria and the Gaza Strip will be the base for Palestinian radicalism and Soviet expansionism against Israel, Jordan, and then further south towards the oil fields of Arabia and Iran.

There is certainly no place to see in all of this a positive PLO contribution to regional peace. This soberly-drawn scenario makes one ask rather desperately: on whose side is America when it seeks to legitimize the PLO and improve its image? Henry Kissinger, in an interview before "Face the Nation" in Sept. 1979, argued

against the move to bring the PLO into the negotiations, considering that this will bring them to
a standstill. Moreover, it would strengthen radical Arab elements and indulge the Soviet appe-
tite to disrupt the peace talks or, alternatively,
allow the Russians to determine their direction.
This critique of the dominant Washington conception is grounded solidly in the trends of international politics, regional alliances, and Palestinian-PLO aspirations. It cannot go unanswered
for long. History will see to that.

(2) The Soviet Threat

The dominant Establishment conception has
come to recognize — particularly with the new
Reagan administration — the growing Soviet
threat to American interests in the Mideast region. This has taken some time, but finally — in
spite of Brzezinski's habit of minimizing the
Russians' global drive — voices are being heard
calling on the West "to cope with Soviet activism
and expansionism in the Middle East."[22] With its
proxy wars fought by Ethiopia in the Horn of
Africa, South Yemen in the Arabian Peninsula,
and the PLO in Lebanon, USSR influence is en-
circling the area in general and the Persian Gulf
oilfields in particular. Noteworthy in this respect
is the fact that regimes identified as pro-Western
have fallen more and more under Soviet influence. Two examples concern Kuwait and North
Yemen both of whom have benefited by the

transfer of Soviet arms and have as well followed
Soviet diplomatic guidelines. In the Arab Summit held in Fez, Morocco in November 1981
both these countries joined Arab Rejectionist
Front states, like Libya, Syria and Iraq, in veto-
ing the Saudi initiative of Prince Fahd. Reminiscent of the strategic semantics of Cold War politics, Soviet regional penetration in the Middle
East outflanked America's so-defined Arab ally.

In the Mediterranean zone what used to be an
"American lake" of the Sixth Fleet is now more
and more under the shadow of Soviet naval
power. The Russians have facilities in Libya, off
the Algerian coast, anchor at Malta, Crete,
Egypt, and Syria. The US bases in Turkey are
jeopardized by strained relations between the
two countries; homeporting privileges in Greece
ended in 1975; the American communication
network left Cyprus in 1974; and the headquarters of the tactical Air Force moved out of Spain
in 1974 as well. The trend throughout the entire
region is towards a strengthening of the Soviet
position and a weakening of the American
presence.

The Soviet naval and air threat to US power is
a grave matter in the Mideast. While a nuclear
stalemate of some kind may nullify that category
of weaponry, the Russian conventional military
superiority suggests that US policy in the region
will be handcuffed severely by this incontrovert-
ible fact. Fearing USSR power will freeze US

maneuverability and force concessions out of the Americans.[23] It can also, as in the hostage episode in Iran, bring the Administration to its knees. Muslim fanaticism and Russian power are formidable obstacles to US freedom of action in the sensitive gulf zone.

In August 1979 the Department of Defense and the CIA held a seminar on US global strategy and played two simulation games on confrontation scenarios in the Middle East. An observer commented as follows:

> In one, it was demonstrated that if tomorrow the Soviets send their Cuban mercenaries into Saudi Arabia, we could do nothing about it. In the other, if the Soviets' Mediterranean fleet became aggressive in the Middle East, all our Mediterranean — or Sixth — Fleet could do is sit passively by and watch.[24]

These hypothetical outcomes did in fact seem close to real-life developments: compare US intervention in the Lebanese Civil War in 1958 with its passive disposition since the outbreak of civil strife in 1975. In the first instance the American policy was designed to strengthen the Maronite community; in the second instance the Christians have been abandoned to PLO Muslim forces and their Soviet supporters. The basis of US passivity in the 1970's is due, in part, to the relative growth of Russian power in what was previously an American sphere of influence.

According to a popular Washington belief, the continued Arab-Israeli conflict was the source of Soviet penetration of the Mideast region. To resolve the conflict was to bolster America's position by denying access to the Russians. John Connally felt that the persistence of this deadlock led the Arabs to depend on the Soviets for weaponry in their struggle against Israel. Without this need, he surmised, they would throw the Russians out — 'just as Sadat did'.[25] George Ball similarly saw Soviet involvement due to Moscow's opportunity to exploit situations of discontent and strife. The conclusion drawn was obvious: the global expansion of USSR influence was a product of a regional issue which, if solved, would no longer offer the Russians a basis for activism in the Mideast. This view underestimated the independent forces driving the Soviet Union into the region making the Arab-Israeli conflict a cause, but more importantly a pretext, for its widespread thrust into the area. There is in this view a touch of American guilt feelings based on the failure of the United States since 1948 to bring about a resolution of the local regional conflict. That alleged failure opened the door to Russian penetration (witness the Czech arms deal to Egypt in 1955, for example). Yet, to take a phrase from Eugene Rostow, it is wholly characteristic of American decency, innocence, and puritanism to blame what goes on in the world on the US and to assume that other nations share her good intentions. This inward-looking self-examination can blind people to "the central driving factor in world politics since 1945" — Soviet expansionism.[26]

It follows from this conception that the USSR should be involved in the effort at peace-making between the Arabs and Israel. The Brookings report felt that 'the Soviet Union is increasingly annoyed at being left on the sidelines' since Kissinger vaulted onto the diplomatic stage in 1973. Its close relations with Syria and the PLO give the Soviet Union a considerable capacity to complicate or block the realization of a comprehensive settlement; its active participation is therefore a US interest of the first order. Peace, we recall, will undermine the Russian role in the Mideast and the Russians themselves will paradoxically help the Americans to bring this about.

This entire approach ignores what William Quandt has recently realized that the payoffs for the Soviets are bigger from other Middle Eastern issues than the Arab-Israeli conflict. Persian Gulf instability and oil will bring them more benefits with much less effort and risk. The conflict itself becomes irrelevant to Soviet ambitions and superpower competition, and America must seek a different response to the Russian menace.

The development of détente was seen as the peaceful diplomatic method of containing the

Soviet Union by compensating her with certain concrete benefits like technological information, trade, and a recognition of post-World War II Russian gains in Europe. Western wishful thinking has had difficulty fathoming the determined communist commitment to a world vision where American capitalist economics and liberal democracy are smothered in the totalitarian Marxist age of socialist rule everywhere. The Soviet Union, since the inauguration of détente and the signing of SALT I in 1972, continues to spend 50 per cent more than the United States on strategic and conventional arms. Linked to Russian activism in the Arab world and Persian Gulf zones, it is disturbingly blatant that détente alone does not have the capacity (I almost said 'teeth') to arrest Soviet growth, expansionism, and threat to Western interests in the Mideast.

A third and related American answer has focused on the buildup of US power in the region in order to physically prevent a further penetration by the Russians. Arms control agreements with the Russians do not nullify the need for American armaments' development. President Carter himself stated in a speech on February 20, 1980 that 'SALT II is not a panacea. It is a supplement, not a substitute — for a strong defense'. Yet, we recall, US defense spending was 9.4 per cent of the GNP in 1968 but just 5.8 per cent by 1976. Now the trend has been somewhat reversed. President Reagan has increased defense spending, accelerated production of strategic military items like cruise missiles, and seeks to strengthen the NATO alliance for Atlantic regional security. Specific to the Persian Gulf area is the American intention to establish a sizable military force capable of rapid deployment in Middle East crises, no doubt those particularly relating to threats to oil supplies. Yet this force is scheduled to be fully prepared only in 1985.

The dominant response in this overall view to increase American power is the need for a maritime strategy that promises the most military gains with the least political risks. At the moment the US has naval access to two ports in the Persian Gulf area: in Bahrein and at the Masirah Island base off the Oman coast. In the Indian Ocean Diego Garcia is available as well for docking purposes. The Atlantic Council report recommended 'raising overall US naval strength to make possible the increased presence in the Indian Ocean' of sufficient forces to meet American and Western needs there. Other suggestions have focused on the requirement of a US naval base on Masirah Island and expanded facilities at Diego Garcia. These various proposals have in common a realization that America must *on her own* act in a forthright manner to strengthen her military preparedness in the Mideast region to counter Soviet power and threats against Western interests. This in itself is the beginning of a credible response to the problem based on a realistic understanding of its magnitude.

The fourth, and last, American approach coming from the Washington Establishment sees in close ties with key Arab-Muslim states the key to preserving US interests in the Middle East. In a sense, it has long been State Department policy to emphasize the military value of Arab states, even though US military circles showed little enthusiasm. In the mid-1940s the Department of War downplayed the security role of Saudi Arabia while the State Department talked of a US "national interest" there. State, more than War, pushed for an air base at Dhahran. The diplomats, not the generals, seemed more influential in military policy-making. The recent sale of F-15 planes to Saudi Arabia seems similarly to be motivated by other than security considerations, such as economic dependency and political cooperation.[27]

American reliance on major Arab-Muslim states to keep the Russians out of the Middle East, or minimally restricted to their present positions, involves particularly three countries which will be examined separately:

Iran: A lesson from history

While recent events in Muslim Iran have eliminated her as an American ally, the traditional reliance on the Pahlavian dynasty illustrates the conceptual paradigm of Washington in an ideal, not always realistic, form. This approach was formalized by the 1969 Nixon Doctrine that assigned Iran a key role in the protection of the Persian Gulf, through which about 50 per cent of the Western World's oil passes. Sharing a 1200-mile border with the Soviet Union and aware of traditional Russian designs on Iran, the Shah's regime sought American support to thwart any Kremlin design against its southern neighbor. Iran became a member of the CENTO Western alliance system and developed into the strongest military power in the Persian Gulf region. US military assistance was a vital factor in this development.

It is worth stressing initially the key role foreign military aid has played in American policy planning. Arms have been used as a means of cementing relationships as a first goal, and as providing the tools to repel foreign — Soviet/communist — aggression as a second related goal. From 1973-78 Iran ordered $19 billion of US arms as the yearly figure rose consistently for arms actually purchased. The Iranian defense budget climbed from $1.2 billion in 1970 to $9.5 billion in 1976, from 8 per cent of its GNP to 14 per cent.[28] The flood of oil revenues in the 1970's was allocated to arms' purchases in an apparent effort to achieve the above-noted aims: alliance-building and repulsion of threats to the regime. A symbolic indication of the special American interest in Iran was demonstrated by the provision of the Phantom-F4 plane to the Shah's regime in 1968 — the first country outside of Europe to get it. As the Number One Western obstacle to Soviet penetration of the Persian Gulf, particularly following the British withdrawal in 1968 from the gulf itself and from Aden in 1971, Iran was armed solidly to repel possible foreign attack and organized through the SAVAK secret police to counter potential domestic insurrection.

However, US arms transfers worth more than $15 billion since 1950 and about 30,000 Americans serving in Iran could not prevent either the Soviet takeover of the Afghanistan regime in 1978 or the Khomeini upheaval that ultimately eliminated the Shah's rule in 1979. Nor did the US-Iran relationship restrain the sharp rise of oil prices in the 1970's, an OPEC-OAPEC blackmail that the Shah fully took part in.

Saudi Arabia: A lesson from futurology

The most 'special relationship' America has had with any Arab country has no doubt been with the Saudis. The single major location of oil reserves so far discovered and traditionally opposed ideologically and religiously to Soviet communism, Saudi Arabia became a most natural and vital US interest over the years since the 1940's. Regional security needs will assure, according to Emile Nakhleh, that Saudi Arabia remain "a cornerstone of American foreign poli-

cy in the Middle East."[29] While oil has been the
foundation of the US-Saudi linkage, the US administration has consistently tried to strengthen
the desert kingdom's military capacity. In fact,
approximately 90 per cent of Saudi's arms purchases are from the United States and her military budget has been rising sharply in recent
years (by 22 per cent, for example, from 1973 to
1974-5); again, like Iran, Saudi oil money has
been invested in military expenditures. In 1980
alone the Saudis budgeted 20.7 billion dollars to
amass an arsenal of weapons that exceed Saudi
know-how and needs and whose only realistic
future use would be in an Arab military adventure against Israel.

The US has about 30,000 of its citizens in Saudi Arabia, with approximately one-third active
in military endeavors. This figure may grow in
light of the American decision in 1978 to supply
60 F-15 jet fighters to the Saudis. While Saudi
Arabia is surrounded by a number of rather problematic regimes — Southern Yemen, Iraq, and
Ethiopia — its strategic location near the Persian
Gulf and its reach into the Indian Ocean and the
Horn of Africa place it in a variety of important
regional positions. To fulfill such a security function in accord with American expectations, the
Saudis annually have purchased approximately
$4 billion worth of military arms and services
from the US.[30] The Saudi weapons' requests include 150 planes, 300 tanks, 440 artillery pieces,

and 9000 missiles. The 1981 AWACS deal worth over 8 billion dollars alone stressed America's commitment to Saudi security. As the ring of danger has been tightening around her, Saudi Arabia has provided military aid to Northern Yemen and financial assistance to Somalia — states contending with Soviet-supported Southern Yemen and Ethiopia, respectively.

The Atlantic Council document recommends that America support 'a constructive Saudi role in maintaining security on the Arabian Peninsula and in general areas of the Red Sea and of the Persian Gulf'. This is critical due to the fact that 'the basic common interests are strong' between the two countries. Nevertheless, it should not be forgotten that the Saudis imposed a total oil embargo on the United States on October 20, 1973 and that they have not ceased to support an extremist, pro-PLO version of an Arab-Israeli settlement that is not consistent with Washington's approach. Beyond that, the monarchical Saudi regime has shown signs of internal weaknesses that make its role as a US ally a most problematic political proposition as time goes by.

Egypt: A lesson from insight

President Sadat, after assuming power in 1970, shifted Egyptian policy in a pro-Western direction and linked it closely with American goals in the Mideast region. The ejection of the Soviets in 1972 made an Egyptian-US dialogue possible and, later, effective in developing a shared concern about Russian penetration of the area. In order to cultivate this new relationship the administration became an active agent in Israel-Egypt talks following the 1973 war; more significantly, Washington came to openly adopt the Egyptian conception on various outstanding differences between Israel and Egypt after they entered into intensive peace negotiations in 1977. The target of their joint efforts was Israel; the victim was to be, in addition to Israel, the Soviet Union.

US arms credits to Egypt worth $1.5 billion in 1979 attested to the qualitatively new links between the two states, as various sophisticated American military items began arriving in Egypt. In addition, between 1975-1981 American bilateral economic assistance including food aid amounted to close to 6.5 billion dollars. The fall of the Shah, Soviet penetration of the Horn and military take-over of Afghanistan, made Egypt a special link in what was a threatened US security network in the Middle East. The proposed new American striking force, it was reported in early 1980, may utilize the Egyptian port Mersah Matruh; joint military maneuvers by the two countries have already taken place, as Pentagon officials became rather frequent visitors to the land of the pyramids. With Iran lost, Saudi Arabia losing some national confidence, Egypt has become a primary American regional interest.

Assistant Secretary of State Harold Saunders, in a statement to the House subcommittee on Europe and the Middle East on February 7, 1980, described Egypt as 'one of the key nations of the Middle East for the remainder of the century'. Opposed to USSR activism, favoring a peaceful approach to the conflict with Israel, and in possession of a large military establishment, Egypt has turned into a major American interest in the tense region. The administration consequently advocated supplying large quantities of arms to Sadat's regime. It nonetheless should be recalled that Egypt has used its army to fight Israel during the last 32 years and has not denied that it might do so again ('...if Israel would attack Syria, the Camp David Accords would not prevent Egyptian support for her Arab sister-state...'). As well, the Sadat about-face with the Russians in 1972 should be a warning that a radical shift from a pro-US to an anti-US policy is not impossible, but a practical matter that Egypt would consider if national interests so demanded.

Having reviewed the major approaches adopted in American thinking to counter the Soviet threat in the Middle East, we shall briefly summarize the alternative conception which acts as a critique on the dominant Washington outlook. Here are the basic assumptions of the dominant view, followed by a critical comment based on the conception associated with the Letter of 170 US generals:

Assumption 1: The Soviet Union derives entry into the Middle East via the Arab-Israeli conflict.

The policy document of the 170 generals outlines the Soviet threat to Western interests in the Middle East without once mentioning the Arab-Israeli conflict. The oil problem has become a Russian opportunity to exploit Mideastern instability more than the problem of the conflict itself. The Western weaknesses in Asia (Iran, etc.) and Europe are linked much more by oil than by Arab-Israeli tension,[31] yet the easy way out for America has been more a kind of 'running away from reality' than a sober confrontation with it.

Soviet penetration of the region precedes the development of the Mideast conflict as testified by the historic aspiration of Moscow to move southward. In the contemporary era that aspiration has been related to the global drive to undermine the very foundations of Western civilization and alter the balance of power in its favor and against the United States. Rather than the Arab-Israeli conflict inducing Soviet interventionist strategies, the expansionist policy of the Soviet Union has purposely utilized the conflict to advance its interests.

Even when the conflict issue is not pertinent the Russians have pushed their way into the Middle East. This is true for the occupation of part of Iran in the 1940's as well as the takeover of Afghanistan in the 1970's. However, while global political considerations have always driven the Soviets to expand their area of influence, communist ideological considerations have sometimes stalled Soviet expansionism *even* when the Arab-Israeli issue was available as a handy excuse to rationalize it. The rise of Nasser to power in Egypt in the early '50's was met initially with reserve by the Kremlin; his was a bourgeois coup, not a socialist revolution. It took the Russians a few years until, in 1955, they acted to take advantage of him to strengthen their position in this key Arab country, against the background of the Arab-Israeli conflict. This example demonstrates that various factors affect Soviet behavior towards the Middle East beyond the conflict itself. Today, more and more, this has become clear with the sharper Russian focus on areas of the region — Persian Gulf, Indian Ocean, African Horn — where Western interests are critically vulnerable to Soviet intervention, and where the Arab-Israeli conflict is of only marginal importance.

Assumption 2: Détente with the Soviet Union will restrain Russian interventionism and achieve stability in the Middle East.

Even before the Soviet invasion of Afghanistan it was clear that détente did not act to prevent superpower competition in the region. Nor did it bring about stability in the context of the Arab-Israeli conflict (witness Soviet behavior in the 1973 war). So long as détente is based rather on American inferiority than superpower symmetry, it will continue to serve as a cloak for Russian activism as in Angola, Ethiopia, South Yemen, Lebanon, Libya, Iraq, and elsewhere. As the Letter of the generals claimed:

> The National Intelligence Estimate, the most authoritative U.S. government evaluation of intelligence data, acknowledges at last that the Soviet Union is heading for superiority — not parity — in the military arena. This represents a complete reversal of official judgements that were a substantial factor in allowing our government to pursue détente and overall accommodation with the Soviet regime.

Détente now begins to look like American appeasement of the Russian bear, whose grasp is reaching to the last bastions of Western strength in the Islamic Middle East — Iran, Turkey, Pakistan, and the Persian Gulf oil-producing states.

Symptomatic of the weaknesses of détente are the controversial SALT treaties to contain the superpower military buildup and the global dangers deriving therefrom. However, the Soviet ICBM development, its Backfire bomber, its naval strength, advances in its MIRV technology, all suggest that SALT is totally inadequate to arrest the critical Russian challenge to America's global position. Daniel Graham, former Director of the Intelligence Agency of the U.S. Pentagon and Deputy-Director of the CIA, considers 'SALT crazy...it is the rock of this bankrupt foreign policy...that is leading the Free World to the edge of irremedial catastrophe'.[32] The immediate implications of this are no more severe than in the Mideast where the Kremlin has fixed its attention on the core of Western vulnerability. There Western interests are most vital, and there Western strength is dangerously lacking.

Assumption 3: American reliance on key Muslim-Arab states in the region can stop Russian expansionism.

The Letter of the generals recommends the formation of a Western coalition of nations to confront the Soviet challenge, but does not include a single Arab state in this proposed bloc. Ray Cline similarly advocates core alliances tied to the United States with "nations strategically linked by common political, economic, and security interests." This 'non-totalitarian alliance' would not include a single Arab-Muslim state.[33] Eugene Rostow refers to the important American alliances which include, besides Western Europe and others, Iran (the only Muslim country mentioned); however, that was written in 1976.[34] Alvin Cottrell and Thomas Moorer, who studied the weakening of the US military base structure in the Mediterranean region, did not consider any reasonable Arab alternatives to the threat to American positions in Turkey, Greece, and elsewhere.[35] In summary: the dominant Washington pro-Arab alliance paradigm is not an axiomatic political truth accepted by all, but a particular view that is challenged on cultural and strategic grounds as inadequate and unreliable. This can be more specifically analyzed by looking at the three Arab-Islamic states noted in the Establishment approach as central to US interests:

Iran:

The conception of Iran as a bulwark against Soviet penetration of the Persian Gulf was a flimsy piece of American reasoning from the start. Living next door to the Russians has usually compelled countries to seek some form of accommodation, docile or otherwise, and has very seldom encouraged open confrontation. This geostrategic reality has often been lost on the mainstream of US policy-makers responsible for both Europe and the Middle East.

The buildup of Iranian arms stocks was incapable of assuring her a credible military deterrent against Soviet activism in the area. It is often the case that developing nations, like Iran, lack the trained manpower to absorb, maintain, and integrate the sophisticated weapons systems supplied by Western countries. Arms supplies, that are not part of a comprehensive and realistic strategy, serve more to offset the US deficit in its balance of payments than to assure an effective response to Russian challenges.

Beyond these considerations, Iran was always more vulnerable to domestic upheaval than Washington considered. In the mid-'70's a Congressional study cited Iran as an alternative location for communication and intelligence facilities then in Turkey.[36] This recommendation became obsolete in just a few years time as the Islamic coup by Khomeini cut ties with the United States. In 1977 a House Staff Survey Mission had dismissed the dangers to the Shah's regime as little more than "irritants".[37] Yet the "irritants" made Iran an even less likely candidate than Turkey for a strategic alliance with America.

Saudi Arabia:

Since the fall of the Shah, the Saudi monarchy seems to be the next likely domino in the elimination of traditional rule in the Persian Gulf-Arabian Peninsula area. Without a broad popular base of support and threatened by the large foreign presence within its borders — about one in four residents is not an indigenous Saudi —the regime fits a feudal model of fragile transitory power on its way out. The pack of Palestinian radicals, South Yemini enemies, Islamic fanaticism, and Russian conspirators together make a lasting Saudi rule improbable. And this without connection to apparently freak occurences like the assassination of King Faisal in 1975.

The recent attack against the Great Mosque of Mecca was only successfully handled when the Saudis received the active military assistance of the French. This demonstrated that the country's welfare is precarious not only in political terms but in military terms as well. The military manpower base is still thin, as loyal Bedouin elements constitute a fraction of the total population of some five million people. In fact, at least three instances are recorded of an attempted coup, one by a segment of the air force in 1969.

There are rumors of a growing American realization that the Saudi regime will not last much longer in spite of earlier assessments, like that by Nakhleh, that no major political upheaval is expected to occur.[38] The country lacks inner social cohesion, political integrity, military capacity, and economic (as opposed to financial) strength. One current story tells of an American effort to convince King Hussein of Jordan to agree to yield his claim to the West Bank (and maybe the East Bank too?) in favor of an indigenous Palestinian Arab-ruled state east of the Jordan River, in return for his family's political restoration in Saudi Arabia from which it was eliminated by Abdul Aziz Ibn-Saud in the 1920's.[39] This extravagant plan, reminiscent of British Imperial king-making days, would at least be realistic insofar as the vulnerability of the present Saudi regime is concerned. It would not assure, however, that an alternative monarchy — that of Hussein's Hashemite dynasty — would overcome all the weaknesses presently undermining the Saudi dynasty of today.

Egypt:

With the fall of the Shah and Saudi Arabia looking shaky, Egypt has become the next and newest cornerstone of US attempts to arrest Soviet penetration of the Middle East. While no Egyptian military engagement in the last 30 years has ended in a clear major success — neither against Israel, including the 1973 war, nor in Yemen in the 1960's — still Egypt does have one of the better armies in the Arab world today. Military efficiency comes with experience, and certainly the many wars fought by Egypt against Israel have provided her with vast experience. However, for reasons that will be noted, America traditionally opposed considering Egypt as a military ally. Former Senator Frank Church, when chairman of the Senate Foreign Relations Committee, declared as late as March 2, 1979 that 'the Congress will not support the Egyptian request to purchase large quantities of arms. The last thing we intend to do is turn Egypt into a military giant of the Middle East'. However, the Carter administration and now followed by the Reagan administration began to do exactly what

Congress apparently was very unenthusiastic about — at least until recently.

Yet the role of Egypt to prevent Russian expansionism is dependent on political as well as on military factors. An American-Egyptian alliance of any lasting quality will have to overcome a traditional Egyptian suspiciousness of the West which has, at times, reached very hostile proportions. Sadat himself once wrote: 'Western civilization and its heritage, for which Europe and America so much fear, live only on the debris of the East and would not flourish if they had not sucked its blood.' This historical antipathy suggests that an authentic meeting of American-Egyptian minds may be beyond the reach of Washington. What remains is to base the relationship on pragmatic grounds of shared interests.

So long as Egypt can benefit politically, economically, and militarily from close ties with the United States, it is likely to maintain its present policy orientation. Yet, as the history of the Egyptian-Russian relationship suggests, Egypt will cut ties with America when it no longer finds the Egyptian-American relationship of positive benefit. This is legitimate in terms of Egypt's national interest and is only what any other country would do; nevertheless, it clarifies the limits and highlights the precariousness of basing US interests on the regime in Egypt.

Today Egypt is attacked by Arab regimes and

threatened by domestic opposition forces for its
move to normalize relations with Israel. With
little concrete economic development, an over-
loaded bureaucracy that cannot make the country much more efficient than backward India,
and a power base that rests uneasily on the support of the army — Mubarak's rule may soon
look as shaky as that of Saudi Arabia. Alternatively, Mubarak upon taking office moved to
strengthen his personal standing by indicating
Egypt's desire to solve the outstanding differences with the Arab world, much of which is identified as pro-Soviet leaning Arab Rejectionist
states; he also legitimized anti-Camp David
groups within Egypt. Peace with Israel even if it
lasts, though the doubts grow daily, will not assure internal progress; nor will the army's satisfaction with territorial gain without having to
fight Israel guarantee long-term support for the
present regime. The weaknesses that eventually
brought down the Shah and may bring down the
Saudi dynasty could bring about the same end in
Egypt. The role of the Soviet Union may be critical in this context, and its role could be of two
very different, even contradictory, varieties: an
estranged USSR, since its 'expulsion' in 1972,
may collaborate with Libya, the PLO, and others
to bring down Mubarak and end his relationship
with the United States; or a still friendly USSR,
working secretly with Mubarak behind America's back, may assure that the recent rendez-vous

with Washington will always remain — with Egypt's full consent — of marginal significance compared to the more profound relationship between Moscow and Cairo. Heads the Russians win, tails the Americans lose.

To summarize: the Arab-Islamic states are generally too unstable politically, underdeveloped economically, unreliable militarily, and unbalanced religiously to make of them sound partners in an American effort to repel the Soviet threat in the Middle East. The logic of Official Washington founders on the fabric of Arab society, culture, and politics which are very different from what many Western observers believe they are. Divorced from the Middle Eastern reality, American policy interests are not fulfilled: Soviet influence continues to grow and an adequate US response has hardly yet been conceived.

(3) The Oil Threat

The dominant American conception holds that a resolution of the Arab-Israeli conflict and the containment of the Soviet danger would, each in its own way, remove the threat of interrupted oil supplies flowing to the West. It is now recognized that America's interests in Middle East oil make the Persian Gulf area a critical priority, perhaps even more so than a resolution of the Arab-Israeli conflict itself. This was implied in a speech by former Secretary of Defense

Harold Brown to the New York Council on Foreign Relations on March 6, 1980, and this theme has been echoed by senior Reagan officials like Secretary of Defense Casper Weinberger and former Secretary of State Alexander Haig.

For the most part, however, the two problems — oil and the conflict — are seen to be related and interdependent. The key elements in what has become a powerful lobby presenting this thesis are a bloc of manufacturers, banks, oil companies, weapons manufacturing firms, and a long list of public relations' enterprises, legal consultants, business advisers, and political figures from the Washington scene who work closely with Arab states.[40] Yet the figures for Western dependency on Arab oil support the thesis and make it look quite credible.

At least one third of all oil produced in the world today comes from Arab countries who participate in OPEC and OAPEC. Saudi Arabia is the major oil-producer, providing about one quarter of the world's oil and possessing the largest reserves accounted for. For the United States, with its own oil and other energy supplies, reliance on imported oil for domestic consumption reaches about 45%; of that figure, approximately 25% of US oil imports come from Saudi Arabia, though only 17% of US fuel consumption comes from the Persian Gulf zone. In comparison, before the Khomeini regime cut off oil exports to America, Iran provided only six per cent of all US oil imports. For Western Europe and Japan the figures are much more overwhelming: 60% of European fuel consumption derives from imports from the Persian Gulf, while Japan purchases 90% of her oil needs from the Middle East — veritably, much of the industrial West is dependent on imported Arab oil. To assure its steady flow, it may indeed *seem* necessary to satisfy Arab demands on the political issues involved in the Arab-Israeli conflict.

The three documents that form the reference point to this overall discussion all agree that a threat to the uninterrupted flow of oil from the Mideast to Western countries is a most real danger since 1973. Yet the difference in tone from the Brookings report of 1975 to the Atlantic Council paper of 1979 is instructive in appreciating the gravity of the matter as perceived over the years. After all, the latter paper is called "Oil and Turmoil". It deals in depth with the energy crisis, the need to develop Western-OPEC relations on a foundation of accommodation, and the necessity for America in particular to cultivate cordial ties with the Arab-Islamic community. This document does not focus specifically on the Arab-Israeli conflict, and this is a healthy conceptual departure with the rising oil prices lurking in the Western consciousness. Yet, while the wider perspective is vital to a realistic approach to *all* of America's challenges, there is in the Atlantic Council paper — along with the emphasis on oil — a much closer identification with the Arab position regarding the conflict than was apparent in the Brookings report. In here lies the linkage of oil and the conflict that the dominant Washington paradigm rests upon.

On April 23, 1980 the Council of Europe recognized the legitimacy of 'Palestinian self-determination' as part of a comprehensive Middle East peace solution. This was the first major international body to formally identify the Palestinian Arabs in political, rather than refugee, terms and is designed to lead to a change of Resolution 242 in this spirit. The Western Europeans are hoping that this policy initiative will assure them the safe flow of Arab oil.

On the very same day as Europe called for 'Palestinian self-determination' and PLO-Israel mutual recognition, Saudi Arabia recalled her ambassador from London and was reported considering cutting off oil shipments to Britain, which purchases fifteen per cent of her oil needs from the Saudis. The reason for this grave development in British-Saudi relations had nothing to do with the Arab-Israeli conflict or the Palestinian question. The source of the problem lay elsewhere: an English-produced film called "Death of a Princess" told the story of a Saudi princess accused of marital infidelity in 1977 who was killed by the authorities in a public display (her lover was beheaded). The screening of the film in England aroused the outrage of the Saudis who considered it a gross intrusion into internal Saudi affairs by presenting them as barbaric murderers. The impugned Arab public image took political revenge on the British, perhaps as a first step to imposing economic sanctions. One is puzzled by the naiveté of the Council of Europe for assuming that it can guarantee the flow of oil by bowing down on the Palestinian altar and burning incense at the feet of Arafat & Co. The Arabs, apparently, have other ideas about how mankind should satisfy their sensitivities. West-Arab relations have a profound cultural dimension beyond the obvious economic one and this point has been ignored to the detriment of the British, in the above case, in an ignoble and insulting fashion. From the Arab political point of view, the freedom of the media and open expression of ideas are not more treasured aspects of Western civilization than Saudi honor; and the fact that the British government did not prevent the screening of the movie must imply, for the Saudis, that it did not want to.

It would be amiss not to mention that two months later, in June 1980, the EEC issued the 'Venice Declaration' that formally and directly recognized the PLO. Still, the dominant American belief is that Arab oil can be guaranteed by a full resolution of the Arab-Israeli conflict. In this manner the Arabs use an economic weapon to achieve a political goal. Senator McGovern once said that if a comprehensive Mideast peace is realized that would include Palestinian self-determination, then "the threat of another oil embargo would all but disappear..."[41] All of this may imply that the Palestinian issue is so central for the Arabs that they are willing to bring Western civilization to its knees in order that 'justice' be accorded their brothers. It also may imply that the West truly believes this to be so; however, as Nietzsche once noted, "what convinces is not necessarily true — it is merely convincing."[42] It is nonetheless true that the 1973 oil embargo was connected with the Arab-Israeli War when American military aid to Israel provided the Arabs with not ... a reason ... but: an excuse.

While resolving the conflict has been the dominant focus of Western thinking to assure oil supplies, various economic solutions have been presented to protect Western societies from an excessive dependency on Arab-producing countries. The Atlantic Council recommends the development of alternatives to Middle East oil — perhaps Alaska, the North Sea, Mexico, and elsewhere — plus energy conservation programs. Lowering domestic rates of consumption and thus diminishing imports of oil has been advanced by a number of analysts, such as Professor Dankwart Rustow, and had been a feature of the Carter approach to the oil problem.[43] Other suggestions call for greater efforts at oil exploration in Asia, Africa, and Latin America — as well as in the United States itself — to diversify sources and loosen the Arab noose around the neck of the West.[44] A report in *Business Week* from August 10, 1981 documented the tremendous oil wealth in West African countries like Nigeria, Gabon, the Ivory Coast and others that have the potential to provide a large part of Western oil needs in the coming years. The Africans in the 1980's will at least partly diminish the oil star that burned like a torch for the Arabs in the 1970's.

There was a time when former Secretary of State Henry Kissinger warned the Arabs that another oil embargo might force America to respond with military intervention in the area of the Middle East. In February 1978 Defense Secretary Harold Brown did in fact declare that oil in the Persian Gulf region is an American and NATO security interest that would be defended against any hostile action and that line of thought is central to the strategic thinking of the Reagan administration. Yet this military possibility has been precluded, for the most part, by political considerations of cultivating amiable relations with the Arab-Islamic world. And the key to that is the resolution of the Arab-Israeli conflict assisted by active American mediation.

It is now appropriate to summarize some major assumptions that underlie the dominant American conception regarding oil and political issues in the Middle East, and present a critique of this conception that provides a different understanding of these problems:

Assumption 1: Arab oil policy is used for the political purpose of affecting the future of the Arab-Israeli conflict.

The fascinating study by J.B. Kelly, *Arabia, The Gulf and the West*, illuminates the Arab-Muslim world's contempt for the West, its powerful urge to 'punish' the Europeans for their past 'imperialist guilt,' and the political purpose of using oil as a weapon to affect the foreign policies of Western governments towards the Arab-Israeli conflict. Arab economic coercion has been met by a shameful lack of Western political will. Yet overwhelmed by the apparent connection between oil and politics, the West has given insufficient attention to the fact that Arab oil policy is also determined by basic economic considerations. Cutbacks in oil production in Iran and Saudi Arabia in recent years had nothing to do with the Arab attempt to force a solution favorable to themselves regarding the Mideast conflict with Israel. While Iranian production dwindled due to internal chaos, Saudi output was manipulated to tighten the market and to keep pricing initiative in the hands of OPEC.[45] With prices rising at very fast rates, smaller levels of production did not mean lower revenues: 3.5 million Iranian barrels produced daily in 1979 earned more than did 5.6 million barrels of daily output in 1978. OPEC made $100 billion a year in the mid-70's and $200 billion in 1979.[46] Anyway you look at it, the ten of thirteen OPEC members which are predominantly Arab-Muslim states are earning a lot of money in sound, though harsh, economic ways.

OPEC policy-making is based largely on economic brinkmanship designed to keep oil supplies just short of demand, or fairly even with it. Guido Bruner, the EEC's energy commissioner, considers the Palestinian issue totally irrelevant to Arab oil policy; oil revenues have become so important for countries like Saudi Arabia that the potential for exploiting this tremendous source of wealth will not be abandoned, even if the West made a major political gesture to the Palestinians.[47] This point is confirmed by Saudi Minister of Petroleum, Sheikh Yamani, who divulged in a lecture at the University of Riyadh in August 1978 that it was not the October War, but an economic decision crystallized by the OPEC ministers two months before the war broke out that led to the drastic rise in the price of oil. The new situation was brought about by the economic opportunity provided by the oil wealth in Arab hands. A different yet related explanation of the embargo — though consistent with the argument that economic motives are the root of Arab uses of oil — notes that technical hitches in the oil wells brought Saudi Arabia to join the embargo and their repair led to the end of its involvement.[48]

Another major general consideration in the Arab use of oil as a weapon relates to the economic situation prevalent in the West. Cutbacks in production are often a function of an economic slowdown in the West: oil production increases when the West recovers. Yet the Arab-Israeli conflict is nonetheless used as a political excuse for Arab behavior, but this has little to do with the real considerations behind their policies.

The proof of the political pudding came in early 1982. From the Arab viewpoint there was no major "progress" towards a resolution of the Arab-Israeli conflict, as no major Arab country joined with Egypt in the Camp David process. Nonetheless, the glut in the world oil market started to bring prices down and OPEC nations experienced a decline in their balance of payments. Mr. Philip Werleger, a Yale University professor, predicted that a barrel of oil might eventually cost $20, down from the present price of $34. It was becoming very clear that oil was fundamentally an economic issue. It follows logically that, even if the Arab-Israeli conflict was resolved, oil would remain the economic issue it is — for better or worse.

Assumption 2: Oil supplies to the West will be assured if the Arab-Israeli conflict is fully resolved.

It follows from the above analysis that problems in oil supplies will not end even if and when the conflict is terminated. Petrocratic tyranny will continue to dominate the global oil scene based on the power — economic and political —that has accumulated in the hands of the OPEC-OAPEC states. Frank Zarb, of the Federal Energy Administration in Washington, considered a possible disruption of oil supplies totally unconnected to the Arab-Israeli conflict, when he testified before a Senate committee in June 1976.[49] A similar judgment was expressed by Professor Fred Singer when he identified the joint OPEC/USSR front against the West on the oil question.[50] We recall that the Russians encouraged the Arab oil embargo against the West in 1973.

Wishful thinking is unfortunately and dangerously sometimes a factor in policy-making and in forecasting future eventualities. In the case of eliminating the oil problem by solving the Mideast conflict there is definitely a note of unfounded optimism in American analysis that underestimates that the two issues may be largely unrelated to each other. Arab propaganda and psychological warfare have created the belief that the connection between the two issues is real and logically demands Western conciliation of Arab feelings. Yet a variety of factors may disrupt the smooth flow of oil even if the conflict is resolved: Soviet intrusion in the gulf area; PLO-

Palestinian intervention in Saudi Arabia (60 per cent of the workforce in ARAMCO is of Palestinian origin); or sober economic considerations leading Arab producers to supply less oil when their financial and planning outlooks compel this. It will always be a good idea to try and solve the Arab-Israeli conflict, whatever one's motives are. However, this is not the same as believing that solving the conflict will assure oil to the West.

Assumption 3: American dependency on Arab oil should not hide the common interests that bind the two sides.

Emile Nakhleh has written that "oil is the underpinning of American-Saudi relations."[51] Consistent with this is the view that the two countries share more in common than differences that split them apart. Neither country would benefit from a sharp rise in the oil price: America might then buy less and Saudi would earn less. Embargoes too are not in their interest, nor is exacerbating the overall economic-industrial situation in the West. A socially weakened Western Europe, following a stop in the flow of Arab oil, would prepare the ground for radical political forces to undermine the democratic regimes. That could lead to communist insurrection and Soviet penetration — in Italy, France, and elsewhere —what neither the Saudis nor the Americans desire.

Nevertheless, the common interests, break

down rather quickly. Professor Morris Adelman
has written as follows:

> There is no basis for an agreement be-
> tween consuming and producing na-
> tions... In point of fact, we have nothing
> to offer Saudi Arabia and its partners,
> and vice versa. We must give them mil-
> itary protection regardless of what they
> do, hence, they need give us nothing for
> this; we have no bargaining power.[52]

What remains is a purely self-interest orientation
impelling both sides of the relationship. America's constant demand for maximum OPEC output at the lowest price is not always or equally
the Saudi priority as well. In fact, a recent report
indicated that even factions within the Saudi
royal family consider the US position damaging
to the producing states.[53]

From the American point of view the danger
of Arab financial power within America proper
is a threat to her national independence in economic and political terms. With $80 billion in
Saudi foreign currency reserves the United States
has to contend with this major fact in its financial planning.

In Saudi Arabia and in other Arab oil-
producing countries, America's economic welfare is precariously dependent on a variety of
rather problematic governments. As Professor
Edward Luttwak warned: 'The prosperity of

Americans and the economic survival of core allies cannot be allowed to depend on the dubious goodwill of transitory regimes, regimes which are neither stable nor progressive.'[54] American-Saudi shared interests may be a euphemism for a US policy of appeasement. Luttwak wisely calls for a formidable public display of an American readiness to act to deter an oil embargo threat or any other danger coming from the Arab-producing states. Saudi Arabia, we recall, was a leader of the oil embargo in 1973.

OPEC is not linked primarily to the Arab-Israel arena but, first and foremost, to the North-South and East-West arenas. OPEC is a powerful base for the developing nations in the southern part of the world to squeeze out of the northern industrial part some of the wealth that the southerners believe was accumulated at their expense. The Black slave episodes and colonial-imperialist rule are still fresh in the memory of Asians and Africans; the Arabs seek revenge in the name of all southerners by utilizing their oil power against a vulnerable American-European belt in the northern half of the world.

In addition, OPEC is a major element in the struggle of the East — Third World Nations and the Soviet bloc — against the West which dominated international politics during the last centuries. With Russian collaboration, OPEC turns into a specific anti-Western instrument to bring the former imperialist powers to surrender their political independence and national honor. That gut urge, plus the economic profits and political stature earned, will motivate OPEC members no matter what happens with the Arab-Israeli conflict. The conflict really begins to seem marginal to the core concerns of OPEC and its Arab leaders whose vision focuses on fundamental historical, cultural, political, and economic issues of global proportions.

The American effort to tie its political conception and national interests with the Arab world has not succeeded to achieve basic American goals. The Arab-Israeli conflict is not fully resolved and Middle East tension suggests that the danger of a future war has not been eliminated. The Soviet threat continues to haunt the US in the region and seems to be closing in on the arc of instability located in the Persian Gulf-Arabian Peninsula zone.

The oil threat too is unresolved and a constant point of Western vulnerability, and there is no sense any longer to deny the connection between the economic hardships that Western Europe is undergoing and that America is beginning to experience with the enormous outlays of money provided the Arab world for oil purchases. Arab wealth is attained at the expense of Western impoverishment. This balance-sheet of American problems indicates that the expectations accompanying the dominant Washington conception on the Middle East have been largely unfulfilled.

Clearly the basic foundation of the US approach has been reliance on the Arab-Islamic world and close coordination with its major countries. From a purely *practical* point of view, US policy-makers have misconstrued the nature of Arab regimes, their lack of stability and reliability, their military ineffectiveness as Western allies, and their unwillingness to closely identify with American ambitions. Yet from a *cultural* or *ideological* point of view, the US-Arab alliance was inauthentic from the start. The OPEC phenomenon is just one startling illustration of this but it is by no means the only expression of the profound gap between the two civilizations: the liberal West and Arab-Islam. In brief, the American-Arab linkage cannot, and ought not, work. The following chapter presents an alternative conception and policy strategy for the United States in the Middle East. We turn now to examine the American-Israeli connection.

Ronald Reagan: American policy-makers downgrade Israel's geopolitical importance as a stabilizing force, as a deterrent to radical hegemony and as a military offset to the Soviet Union. The fall of Iran has increased Israel's value as perhaps the only remaining strategic asset in the region on which the United States can truly rely; other pro-Western states in the region, especially Saudi Arabia and the smaller Gulf kingdoms, are weak and vulnerable.

The Washington Post,
Aug. 15, 1979

CHAPTER 3:

AN AMERICAN-ISRAELI STRATEGIC ALLIANCE

The purpose of this chapter is to present three different features of US-Israeli relations in an effort to capture both their positive and negative aspects. Rather than provide an extended *historical* overview of their multifaceted relationship, this approach will be more *analytical* in focusing on critical dimensions of it. We shall arrive at a juncture that points to the encouraging prospects of a tight strategic linkage between America and Israel that, while based on organically shared values and aspirations, moves towards the closest political and military connection designed to realize their common national interests.

Any possibility of a formidable US-Israeli strategic alignment would call for a radical change in the dominant Washington conception regarding America's Mideast policy. Westerners, in spite of pro-Israel public opinion, have supported the Arab case in the conflict and their version of the manner of its resolution — such as the withdrawal of Israel from territories taken in wars the Arabs initiated — but, beyond that, they have really been captivated by the charming and exotic Arab personality and often repulsed by the coarser Israeli type.[1] Sadat's spell over the American public is just an exceptional instance of this phenomenon which has been widely prevalent ever since the Western powers began to take serious interest in Middle East affairs. An effort to highlight a possible American preference for a close connection with Israel would involve a rejection of the historical pro-Arab thrust in US policy-making as well as overcoming the cultural strain in American-Israeli relations.

The State Department bureaucratic apparatus represents the locus of Washington's traditional view that has been fundamentally unchanging in its attitude towards Zionism and Israel for sixty years. The recruitment of like-minded officials and the maintenance of what could be termed 'standard operating procedures' have assured that the routine pro-Arab slant would not be questioned or challenged by either new kinds of personnel or political approaches. No bureaucratic machine easily strays from its usual path of behavior and this administrative rule has certainly characterized State Department policy towards the Mideast notwithstanding the very different types of personalities who have filled the presidency in the White House. The river follows its course no matter who is trying to adjust its current. The traditional policy approach looks almost like a natural phenomenon that is ineluctable in its force.

A different kind of obstacle to developing a formidable pro-Israel approach lies in the visual difficulty of believing that, somehow, tiny Israel can be a more effective ally of American interests in the Middle East than the Arab-Muslim world with its tremendous territorial expanse, economic resources, and demographic strength. A look at the map of the region highlights Israel's insignificance compared to the land mass occupied by 22 Arab states from the Atlantic to the Persian Gulf. One needs a certain imaginative faculty to conclude that Israel can serve as an effective and credible link in America's strategic network in this critical part of the world, in spite of her lack of territory, resources, and population. Beyond the historical, cultural, and bureaucratic impediments to their alignment, the perceptual difficulty of seeing Israel as potentially more valuable to America than are the Arab states cannot easily be dismissed. It may be a perceptual fallacy to infer strength from size in the Arab case; yet it will require the clearest vision to perceive quality without quantity in Israel's case. What might aid such a vision is the realization that the historic achievements of the Jewish people have been earned by the few against the many.

1) America's Commitment to Israel

The dominant motif in US-Israeli relations has been a public American commitment to the well-being of the Jewish state since its creation in 1948. This commitment has been expressed and reiterated over the years in the most consistent fashion and appears in the Atlantic Council document in spite of the report's primary concern with Western ties to the Arab-Muslim world.[2] This US obligation has been articulated in rather similar language by such politicians as: Henry Kissinger — 'The survival and security of Israel are unequivocal and permanent moral commitments of the U.S.';[3] Harold Brown — 'The U.S. is firmly committed to Israel's security';[4] Adlai E. Stevenson, III — 'The American commitment [to Israel] is, and must remain, unequivocal';[5] and Harold Saunders — 'Our commitment to a secure, free, and democratic Israel is firm...'.[6] This standard American position reaffirmed by President Reagan and other senior administration officials on many occasions suggests that Israel's physical integrity is a vital commitment that Washington intends to uphold.

Support for Israel was forthcoming immediately when the state was proclaimed as President Truman led America as the first interna-

tional power to recognize it. Over the years that
diplomatic support has been maintained and was
actively strengthened when the United States became, in addition to an economic support, a military aid supplier in the 1960's. America's commitment to Israel's security manifested itself in a
dramatic manner by the airlift authorized by
President Nixon during the difficult early days of
the Yom Kippur War. At that time the administration announced a $2.2 billion program in mil-
itary credits to pay for tanks, aircraft, missiles
and other arms sent. Since the war Israel, according to one calculation, received nearly $20 billion
by 1979.[7] It is the near exclusive and massive
American economic and military assistance that
has led some observers, like Senator Ribicoff, to
declare that 'Israel could not have existed and
cannot exist without strong U.S. support'.[8]

This is a dangerous 'double-edged sword' in
the context of the Arab-Israeli conflict. Sadat
had commented that America holds 99 per cent
of the cards in terms of what happens in the
region, being well aware of Israel's grave dependence on Washington's support. In fact, one
of the primary purposes of his peace venture had
been to undermine the US-Israeli relationship
and bring pressure to bear on Israel. Her good
fortune to benefit from the American commitment to her security carries with it the disadvan-
tage of a precarious reliance on US goodwill
which, if eroded by Arab diplomacy, can elimi-

nate one of the most formidable foundations of Israel's very existence. This development can occur at any time the administration decides that America's commitment to Israel harms the country's national interests. Invariably and legitimately, a moral commitment which is of questionable practical value may be abandoned by a responsible government.

The US commitment has asserted itself even when the administration itself has been at odds with Israel on certain issues. When President Nixon momentarily balked at providing certain aircraft to Israel in 1971, a statement signed by 79 senators called for the transfer of such weaponry. Again, in 1975, when the administration was at loggerheads with the Rabin government over a Sinai II agreement and Kissinger announced the need for a major 'reassessment' of American-Israeli relations, 76 senators declared their clear support for Israel. These instances indicated that America's commitment to Israel was deeper than the changing political mood in executive circles; the legislature, representative of the stable national beliefs, serves as a strong bastion of positive feeling towards Israel.

In a speech in Jerusalem on February 9, 1980 Samuel Lewis, the American ambassador to Israel, referred to "an unwritten alliance" that binds the two countries to each other. The US commitment to Israel grows from the shared experiences and values characteristic of the American and Jewish peoples, in the past and present. Ambassador Lewis noted the common pioneering history grounded in the Biblical mythic context of political freedom from unjust rulers; the immigrant enterprise of forging new societies from a multitude of peoples; and the shared dedication to democratic values, the idea of liberty, and a hatred of tyranny and war. He summed up the essence of this relationship in the following way:

> What holds us together is not bargaining positions or cooperative agreements or military supply arrangements or economic aid, but a human and moral bond that cannot be severed.

This formulation is at the root of the 'special relationship' between America and Israel that is not based on crude material considerations between states but, rather, on the more spiritual elements of social brotherhood between nations. Almost 200 years of American presidents and leaders supporting the necessity for a homeland for the Jewish people suggest an altruistic ideological motive in the positive US orientation towards Israel.

It has been suggested that Americans cannot help but support Israel because she is really a mirror-image of what America stands for. To abandon democratic Israel is to reject American democracy. To oppose the pioneering Zionist effort is to disparage America's historical drive westward. Israel is a miniature model of American society and is a living proof of the vitality of the American dream in an era when most peoples, including the Arabs, have followed very different paths. Having found public opinion in 1977 in the United States rather favorable to Israel, Seymour Martin Lipset and William Schneider concluded:

> Israel, it is fair to say, is still seen as a brave, small state, composed of people 'like us', surrounded by wealthy, powerful, hostile neighbors, some of whom cooperate with the Communist world. And the past use by the Arabs of the oil weapon and their forcing up of the price of oil have reinforced the negative image held of them by most Americans.[9]

In recent years, nonetheless, we have witnessed various American administrations criticize Israel for 'illegal' settlement policies in Judea and Samaria, 'aggressive' action towards neighboring Lebanon, and 'illiberal' actions in its dealings with the Arab population in the country. Together these attacks create a negative image of Israel as a country which no longer represents, at least not as purely as in the past, the positive humanitarian and peaceful ideals that used to identify her closely with American life. This development will inevitably erode the bedrock of the US commitment to Israel.

The fragility of American-Israeli ties, as based on Washington's inherent obligation to the Jewish state, reaches a paradoxical breaking-point with the notion of a US guarantee for Israel's security. In itself, it is psychologically debilitating and politically suicidal to accept the idea that a nation's very existence is dependent on the commitment and promise of another state. Israel must be seen as totally unviable if her very survival rests on an American guarantee; this is to openly admit that she lacks the required national elements of political sovereignty and therefore seeks her welfare as a ward, or satellite, of the United States.

The Brookings report considered that a Middle East peace agreement might necessitate the provision of a US guarantee for Israel's security.[10] This recommendation recalled former Senator William Fulbright's proposal in 1970 for an American treaty with Israel to guarantee her security once she withdrew to the pre-1967 borders. The idea lurking behind the guarantee to Israel is an imposed political settlement of the Arab-Israeli conflict. This was rather elegantly expressed in the Brookings study as follows:

> To judge by the experience of the past eight years, it seems evident that the Arab and Israeli governments cannot reach a

settlement in the foreseeable future without strong encouragement from the great powers.[11]

At Camp David in September 1978 President Carter utilized all his powers of persuasion and American leverage on Israel to achieve a peace agreement between Egypt and Israel. Due to US reluctance or Israeli disinterest, talk of a guarantee to Israel has not moved to the practical planning stages. In fact, it is almost precluded so long as the administration continues to base American interests in the Middle East primarily on close ties with key Arab countries.

The notion of a security guarantee now appears as the negative side of the coin countered by the positive side of a genuine American commitment to Israel. Those who offer the guarantee invariably support a complete Israeli withdrawal from all the territories. Denied any semblance of strategic viability or credible defense posture back in the former vulnerable lines, Israel's very survival can no longer be assured except by a US military guarantee. Brzezinski, prior to joining Carter's staff as National Security Adviser, wrote in 1974 that America should provide Israel with a guarantee as she pulls back from all the territories and abandons the Jewish settlements there.[12] The idea of a guarantee begins to look like a pretext to justify pushing Israel back to the '67 borders. While it rationalizes an apparent concern for Israel, it would undoubtedly lack the credibility and capacity to, in fact, guarantee what would then be an unviable state.

From an authentic American commitment we have come to expose a vacuous guarantee, though a straight line leads from the first to the second position. This recalls Hegel's teaching of the master-slave relationship where the superior partner will always find it difficult, if not impossible, to respect the inferior partner in the relationship. In search of recognition the superior member cannot get it from the inferior one; and the inferior, seeking protection and security, will never know for sure whether the superior will continue to provide those goods. The US-Israel relationship based on the American commitment turns out to be an inherently unstable framework from the beginning, though this may only be clear at the end. In 1980, while losing Washington's diplomatic support on key political questions and denied satisfaction on certain weapons' request, Israel still benefits from America's commitment. Yet, like the proposed US guarantee, it is looking more and more abstract and symbolic, not only of American support, but also of a generally deteriorating relationship between the two countries. It is as if the 'commitment' is the "thing-in-itself" with a life of its own in some ethereal realm of reality; in the political realm of reality it is like some phantom entity, less substantiated as time passes.

2) Israel: America's Burden

A constant aspect of the US-Israel relationship, sometimes more or less influential in affecting policy-making, has been a view of Israel as a grave liability to the realization of Washington's goals in the Mideast. Due to 'parochial' considerations like the Jewish vote in domestic American politics, and residual guilt-feelings deriving from the Holocaust, the US has supported Israel since its creation in flagrant disregard of a rational evaluation of how best to secure its own purposes. The moral bond between the two countries is a millstone around America's neck that finally must be thrust off.

The traditional Zionphobia in the State Department led to a policy that favored the value of Arab friendship and the adoption of their version of what the Mideast conflict was really about. America as peace-maker sought to realize an Arab-Israeli settlement that was largely consistent with Arab claims. This was the case in 1953 when the US administration imposed economic sanctions on Israel for having begun to draw on the sources of the Jordan River which flowed southward from Lebanon and Syria. This was the case in 1956-7 when President Eisenhower pressured Israel to withdraw from all of the Sinai Peninsula and the Gaza Strip without having brought Egypt to make a peace agreement with, or even recognize, the Jewish state. This was the case in 1961 when President Kennedy supported the Arab demand that Israel repatriate Arab refugees who fled Israel in the 1948 war and whose return could undermine her national integrity. This was the case in 1970 when America ignored, in spite of repeated Israeli protests, Egyptian infractions of the canal cease-fire agreement. This was the case in 1973 when the US did not condemn Egyptian-Syrian aggression, forced a cease-fire on Israel that salvaged Egypt's territorial gain from the first days of the war, and frustrated Israel's thrust to end the war with a clear sense of military victory. And most of all: since the Rogers proposals of 1969, every administration supports the Arab demand to recover all territories lost to Israel in the Six-Day War of 1967 that would leave Israel — once again — mutilated strategically, particularly with just a 10-mile width straddling the Mediterranean coast. The Tel-Aviv 'statelet' would be unable to survive for very long.[13]

In the 1950's Ambassador Byroade in Cairo, a close friend of Nasser, demonstrated the identity of American-Arab views in an extreme and most disturbing way. He proposed that Israel relinquish her right to *aliya* [Jewish immigration] and thereby manifest her willingness to become a true part of the region. Byroade considered Israel's *Jewish* character inimical to her full integration into the Oriental — i.e., *Arab* — Middle East.[14] This proposal was made at the same time British prime minister Eden was calling on Israel to relinquish the Negev, the southern area of the country, as a means of gaining Arab recognition.

Throughout these years, over a variety of issues, the Americans adopted or supported the Arab view and sought to free themselves from the burden of their relationship with Israel. The wholesome commitment to Israel was compromised by the heavy price Washington had to pay for the friendship of the Arab world. This definition of the dilemma led John Badeau, former American ambassador to Egypt, to write:

> In the context of American foreign policy, Israel thus needs to be viewed as a problem, rather than as an interest... the major premise of American policy in the Middle East cannot be the protection of Israel but must be the protection of American interests...[15]

The contrast between what is perceived as an American "commitment" to Israel and American "interests" in the Arab world is sharp and unchallengeable. The moral commitment cannot — when all is said and done — obligate a policy which might sacrifice Washington's fundamental political and economic interests. The result of realizing basic American interests in the Arab world becomes therefore the abandonment of Israel. The US here agrees to play by the rules as laid down by the Arabs.

General Brown, former Chairman of the Joint

Chiefs-of-Staff, openly referred to Israel in 1976 as a 'burden' that it would be good for America to be free of. Beyond the apparent anti-Semitic dimension to Brown's comments on Jews and Israel, his conviction that Israel is a liability to the United States reflected a certain strategic conception that has guided American policy in the Mideast. This view considers Washington's ties with Israel responsible for complicating and delaying quick resolution of the regional conflict, exacerbating US relations with the Arab world, threatening the steady flow of oil to the West, and inducing a Soviet-Arab alignment that undermines basic American global interests in the region. There is in this formulation a touch of the classic anti-Semitic claim that, were it not for the depravities of the Jew, all would be well. The appearance of a Jewish state in the modern era has apparently not precluded the use, or misuse, of the grotesque stereotype of the Jew — or Israeli — at the root of the world's problems.

The AWACS debate was not clean from certain anti-Semitic smears that characterized the manifold efforts of persuasion used by the administration to assure Congressional support. If the deal had been rejected by the Senate, the responsibility would have been placed squarely on the Jewish lobby in Washington. It is most common for the view of Israel as a political burden to go hand in hand with a very poor understanding of Middle East realities. Typical of this is an article that appeared in the *New York Times* at the height of the AWACS issue written by Orrin G. Hatch of Utah, Vice-Chairman for foreign policy of the Senate Republican Steering Committee, where he wrote:

> How can America obtain military facilities that its Rapid Deployment Force needs to defend Arabian Gulf oil fields if even moderate Arabs continue to point to Israeli "intransigence" on the Palestinian question?

Senator Hatch indicates here his pro-Arab bias and his apparent ignorance of the pro-Soviet trend in Persian Gulf politics, that has about as much to do with the 'Palestinian question' as Soviet aggression in Afghanistan has to do with the 'Hispanic question' in America.

The Gulf Cooperation Council has categorically rejected the idea of any American military presence in the Gulf area and continues to pressure Oman to sever its strategic ties with the United States. America's real burden in the Persian Gulf is contending with Soviet penetration and Arab rejectionism.

This distorted understanding of American-Israeli relations draws upon two very different though complementary notions in order to invalidate the links between the two countries. Employing a *rational* argument, the US is encouraged to abandon its sentimentality to the Jewish state, recognize the grave financial, political, and economic costs inflicted on American interests, and adopt a cool-headed pro-Arab policy without any limitation whatsoever. In a recent report submitted to the Joint Chiefs-of-Staff of the American army Israel was portrayed as a country that is expected to wither away in the coming decade. It lacks the necessary requirements to be a viable ally of the United States in the Middle East.[16] It cannot serve as a safe economic investment or as a credible military partner. Based on the implications of the recent Camp David Peace Treaty — denied territorial depth, economic (oil) resources, military capacity, and national vitality — Israel does seem to be almost unable to assure its own welfare, and hardly capable of assisting others, like the United States, to realize their national interests.[17]

Added to this argument is an almost *mythic* caricature of the negative role of Israel in the Middle East generally and as responsible for complicating American national interests there particularly. This approach, at once intellectually questionable yet emotionally powerful, conjures up a desperate anxiety regarding the future state of the world if Israel does not allow herself to be saved, in George Ball's phrase, "in spite of herself." This irrational entity, driven by deep historical complexes and one-sided self-interest, can undo any progress towards a more stable and peaceful region unless bound by America's power and logic. It becomes legitimate and necessary, therefore, to cast Israel off in order to save America and sacrifice the Jews (to the wolves?) for the welfare of mankind (and its oil furnaces in the winter). Israel is a burden that cannot be borne any longer. America must act resolutely to incapacitate the dragon by cutting it into pieces (or force it to relinquish the territories) and then watch it slowly die off.

The political logic and mythic imagination impelling this overall approach can ultimately sever any remaining links between the US and Israel and thereby nullify any positive impact that derives from the traditional commitment Washington assumed towards the well-being of the Jewish state. There is good reason to believe that this still is to a large degree the dominant trend characterizing American-Israeli relations as we move into the 1980's. It remains to consider if this trend can be reversed, soon before it becomes too late.

3) Israel: America's Interest

From an historical viewpoint the idea that Israel constitutes a positive and substantial benefit to the United States has been a marginal element in their relationship. Perhaps, because of its difficult past and domestic character, Israel merits US support; yet this suggests that America derives no advantage whatsoever from their relationship. It gives but has nothing to receive from

Israel. This certainly strengthens the belief that the US has key *interests* in the Arab world due to the needs of America. However it has only a *commitment* to Israel due to the needs of Israel which may not at all be identical with those of America. This self-inflicted damage cannot justify itself much longer.

The Memorandum of Understanding between America and Israel, whose future worth is unfortunately still to be clarified, developed nonetheless against a background of a growing recognition of Israel's importance to America's well-being. Former President Carter, in an address to the United Jewish Appeal Young Leadership Conference on February 25, 1980, called America's relationship with Israel as being 'in the moral and strategic interest of the United States.' Edward Kennedy, his Democratic presidential competitor, had referred to Israel as 'our strongest ally in the area' on January 20th the same year. The Reagan camp even more sharply identified the common strategic interests of America and Israel. Richard Allen, formerly Reagan's National Security Advisor, emphasized in an interview to *Politique Internationale* before the US elections that strategic concerns, not just sentiment, bound the two countries together for shared regional concerns. This recent public recognition of Israel as a positive value to America has not, however, been explicated in order to identify the full logical force for this view.[18] The

Brookings report claims that the 'United States has a strong interest in the security, independence, and well-being of Israel', but there is no attempt to articulate in what manner the American interest manifests itself. One wonders whether anything lies behind this kind of declaration more than mere lip-service to an idea which it is decent and fashionable to express but not to be taken too seriously, and certainly not credible enough to be believed.

It has always been recognized that America and Israel share basic values and views on a number of key ideological and political questions: the importance of democracy as a system of government and way of life; opposition to Communism on various grounds — as a form of political life and social system; and desire to repel Soviet expansionism and Arab influence at the global level. Yet these most fundamental shared perspectives do not assure that America can or would secure Israel if dangerously threatened.

Public opinion polls have indicated that much less than a majority of Americans would support sending US troops to save an Israel being over-run by Arab forces. Not inconsistent with this was former Secretary of State Kissinger's statement after the 1973 Yom Kippur War that the United States would never allow the Soviet Union to win a victory-by-arms in the Middle East. But he clarified the reason to Hassanein Heikal that Washington 'could not — either today or tomorrow — allow Soviet arms to win a big victory, even if it was not decisive, against US arms. This has nothing to do with Israel or with you'.[19] Kissinger stresses America's global strategic interests rather than any kind of moral commitment to Israel's welfare. However, in a press conference on December 27, 1973 — Israel still traumatized by the war — Kissinger declared that it was a constant US policy, enjoying bipartisan recognition, 'that the existence of Israel will be supported by the United States'.[20] Yet Kissinger had explained earlier that Washington would intervene to protect *its interests*, not Israel's. In fact Kissinger was allegedly responsible for delaying the US arms airlift to Israel which Nixon eventually ordered. With this episode in mind, one must weigh America's commitment to Israel squarely against America's own national security interests. If the two coincide then America may act resolutely in the Middle East and even claim that this expresses its obligation towards Israel. Yet the true motivation lies elsewhere.

Beyond the question of Washington's willingness to intervene on Israel's behalf is the question of whether the US has the capacity to do so. This question must be considered in the light of Russia's nuclear and conventional superiority over America globally and specifically on NATO's weak southern flank — the Middle East. This has led one analyst to make the following point: the United States would not come to Israel's support against Soviet intervention in a Middle East conflict because it would not risk a Soviet nuclear strike on the American homeland for the sake of three million Jews in Israel.[21] This alleged linkage between an Arab-Israeli war and a potential superpower nuclear conflagration is not unfounded. The key point is, however, that America fears active Soviet intervention in the region because the Russian strategic advantage is so preponderant for geopolitical and purely military reasons. This suggests that the United States, from her point of view, has a faulty understanding of what her true interests are and how best to realize them. It also suggests that Israel, from her point of view, cannot rely on any American commitment, promise, or guarantee to secure her national integrity against Arab and Russian foes in the Middle East. The values and views that America and Israel share may carry with them only a limited payoff capacity — most specifically when the chips are down.

It is of the utmost initial importance to clarify the inherent strengths of Israel before considering her practical value as a strategic ally of the US in the region. The Jewish state enjoys a fundamental political stability that is rooted in a deep national consensus supporting an open, multi-party democratic regime. Its value system assures that Israel will always feel integrally tied to the Western world, no matter what party is in power and no matter what specific policy platform it advocates. The underlying political basis guarantees that Israel be a reliable and dedicated permanent friend of America and this permits long-range strategic planning between the two countries. In contrast Arab regimes, due to their instability, lack of peaceful processes for political change, and very different cultural norms, must be categorized as markedly less trustworthy from America's vantage point. There are examples from Libya in 1969 and Iran in 1979, to mention just two, that illustrate this point.

The educational, scientific, and technological standards of Israeli society put her at the top of Middle East countries and a respectable member of the advanced Western world in these respects. Israel's sophisticated military industries and weapons' development programs make her a vital Western ingredient in NATO's strategic framework and almost a natural partner in that organization's geopolitical and scientific-technological response to the Soviet-bloc countries. It is certainly not necessary to describe the Arab nations as backward in order to appreciate the qualitative edge Israel enjoys over her Mideastern neighbors who are a product of very different historical and cultural traditions than those which established the modern Jewish state.

Israel's military strength is probably its most prominent domestic feature from the perspective of the outsider looking in. The basic fact remains that in five wars — 1948-9, 1956, 1967, 1969-70, and 1973 — Israel has proven its military superiority over Arab armies in spite of their advantages in weaponry, manpower and territory. Yet the qualitative edge of Israel was the critical factor assuring victory against very grave odds. It could also be noted by way of comparison that Israel possesses more combat aircraft and military manpower than a major Western nation like France. And Israel's reliability to fulfill the needs of the American strategic network is undoubtedly greater today than France's. These points are significant in order to paint an accurate picture of Israel as not only a state that takes from the US, but that has something to give. Once it is recognized that Israel has, in the words of Congressman Stephen Solarz, "the most powerful military machine in the Middle East,"[22] it becomes possible to balance the image of Israel as a 'beggar state' with that of Israel as a 'contributing state'. Joseph Churba has argued that Israel has great potential to serve as a permanent and multi-purpose access point in any solid Western security structure, a land route for supplies and as a refueling base, in regional conflicts where major American interests are endangered.[23]

Putting all this together — political stability and reliability, scientific and technological sophistication, and military effectiveness — Israel becomes a tangible and attractive country that can contribute in concrete ways to a Western alliance system. The critical element that forges Israel's modern society into a capable instrument is its high sense of national purpose. Founded on the pioneering dedication of generations and motivated by the Jewish dream of a renewed homeland, Israel expresses the vision of a people whose national regeneration and political freedom stand as the paramount aims of the country. This provides a focus for collective efforts and a measure for state goals. It gives Israel a positive purpose that becomes a much more permanent and galvanizing force in national life than the more negative efforts of many Arab countries in their struggle against Israel over the years. In Israel the society's goal is to build something positive and constructive; in the Arab world the society's goal is negative and destructive for the most part — to bring down the Zionist enterprise after over 80 years of Jewish national work in the Land of Israel. The conflict-ridden feudal societies of the Arab world, lacking social cohesion and national purpose, are internally less viable countries and consequently less reliable states than Israel is.

With the domestic vibrancy of Israel in mind, it now becomes appropriate to sketch the outlines of an American-Israeli strategic relationship. It is the internal foundation within Israel that supports the cooperative efforts of the two countries. We have gone beyond the more spiritual, ideological, and moral affinities binding the United States and Israel to concentrate on the political, technological, and military coordinates of their alignment. This exercise corresponds to a timely piece of advice from the late Professor Hans Morgenthau:

> For Israel to rely upon the continuing strength of traditional emotions would be not an act of policy but of desperation. Israeli statesmanship must try to create competing new interests, such as an American naval base in Israeli waters, that will strengthen the ties between the United States and Israel and counter the forces pulling the United States toward the Arab side.[24]

While Morgenthau realistically looked towards the future, the following instances of American-Israeli strategic cooperation from the past show what has already been achieved in their relationship. This brief review should be counterposed to the summary of Soviet-Arab strategic coordination presented in Chapter 1.

In September 1970, at the height of King Hussein's military campaign against the internal Palestinian-PLO terrorist threat to his kingdom, Washington called upon Jerusalem to deter Syrian aggression and intervention against Jordan. During intense talks between Secretary Kissinger and Israeli Ambassador Rabin, the two countries

coordinated their actions towards the Jordanian
crisis. Weakened within and threatened without,
Hussein requested via the Americans that Israel
carry out an air strike against Syrian tank units if
they advanced deep into the country. President
Nixon had decided that the regime must not fall,
but the only effective and credible way of assuring this was by employing the Israeli forces. The
Meir government agreed to utilize the Israeli
army in order to protect Jordan's national integrity: tank units moved up to the eastern border
and the air force was readied for action. Upon
Hussein's surprising repulse of the Syrian attack
in the north, Israel's deterrent or active assistance was no longer needed. Yet the core point
was America's realization that Israel was its only
staunch ally to stop Soviet-supported Syrian aggression and Soviet-armed PLO forces against
the Western-oriented Jordanian regime. To this
effect Nixon committed the US to intervene
against the Russians (or the Egyptians) if they
moved against Israel. This joint military planning between America and Israel was a significant manifestation of coordinated strategic action, in spite of the fact that no formal defense
pact bound them. It also pointed to the centrality
of Israel at the core of a Western-bloc, Amer-
ican-supported group of nations in the heart of
the Middle East.[25]

The Suez Canal remained closed from 1967,
when war broke out, until 1975 when progress

towards Israeli-Egyptian normalization was taking place. During that eight-year period the Soviet Union shipped massive amounts of equipment via the long route around the Cape of Good Hope to North Vietnamese forces fighting the US army in south-east Asia. This extended distance slowed down arms shipments and weakened the Vietnamese war effort. This extra burden on the Soviet Union and on North Vietnam was of considerable benefit to the United States. The ability of Israel to hold the canal line during the intense artillery barrages by Egypt into Sinai during the War of Attrition from 1969-70 was the paramount reason for eliminating the Suez Canal as the short route for Russian provisions destined for Vietnam. Israel paid a heavy price during this fighting for the canal line: 346 dead and some 1500 wounded. The Russian-trained and supplied Egyptian army was kept at bay and, as a consequence, Israel served America's global interests by inflicting difficulties on the communist battle against the United States in south-east Asia. If Egypt had broken Israel's resistance and crossed the canal, the waterway would have been opened — and then Russia would have derived considerable benefit in its campaign against American forces in Asia.

Over the years Israel has transferred to the United States Soviet-manufactured weapons captured in Israeli military confrontations against the Russian-supplied Arab armies. This intelligence on Soviet planes, missiles, and other war material 'cannot be reckoned in dollar costs' according to General Keegan. He has added that five CIAs could not have provided such critical information that is of great help today to defend NATO's positions against the Warsaw Pact military bloc.[26]

The involvement of Syria in the Lebanese Civil War on the side of the PLO has threatened to establish a Soviet-supported power in what was formerly a Western-oriented Lebanon. The Christian community has succeeded to maintain its minimal survival needs only thanks to Israeli assistance. Israel has provided weaponry and training, and the intermittent Israeli raids against the PLO targets have balanced off Syrian assistance to the PLO forces. It is very conceivable that the Syrian-PLO forces would have together fully assumed national power in Lebanon, were it not for the vital role played by Israel there. In spite of the Western world's abandonment of the Maronites and America's flirtation with the PLO and Syria, the preservation of a viable Christian Lebanon is a basic interest of the Free World. As in Jordan in 1970, so in Lebanon in 1980: Israel forms the axis of Western-bloc nations to prevent a further expansion of Soviet influence in the Middle East. Israel's containment of the PLO and the Syrians in Lebanon helps block the Russian imperial drive southward, all the way to the oilfields in the Persian Gulf zone.

These instances of American-Israeli shared strategic interests have had to force their reality upon US administrations that, at times, sought to deny their telling message.

In 1981 alone Israel acted with determination and force against three of its Arab enemies *all of whom are tightly integrated into Soviet regional alliances.* The Begin government's political and military activism focused on Israel's threatened Eastern Front Rejectionist states: In June Israel destroyed the Iraqi nuclear reactor, the greatest potential threat to Israel's very existence; in July Israel attacked PLO military headquarters in Lebanon, the center of Arab terrorism against Israel's northern population; and in December Israel annexed the Golan Heights, formerly part of Syria and used as a springboard for military aggression against Israel.

These Israeli actions, designed to serve the country's most fundamental security needs, were met with a harsh American overreaction. President Reagan denounced these Israeli steps and 'punished' its staunch Middle East ally by delaying the shipment of contracted aircraft and by suspending the implementation of the Memorandum of Understanding agreed upon a short time before. American pressure to assure Israel's final withdrawal from Sinai reduced Israel's strategic worth and military reach and is exposing her to

powerfully armed and potentially threatening
Arab states on her southern border. In truth,
facing the fact that Egypt had violated the Camp
David treaty in many serious political ways, Israel was perhaps compromising her basic interests with the final withdrawal.[27] It was Ronald
Reagan himself who said on ABC's "ISSUES
AND ANSWERS" on September 11, 1977 that
'no country has ever observed the terms of a
treaty if it suited its national purpose to break
that treaty.'

If properly cultivated, a wide-ranging American-Israeli strategic relationship could deepen
and extend to various critical theaters of potential action. Israel could be the vital agent to
make American power in the region a credible
factor. Note the following areas of Western concern:

The Persian Gulf

It is highly unreasonable to expect any Arab-
Muslim state, such as Egypt, acting to assure the
flow of oil to the West at a time of confrontation
in the gulf zone. This political point nullifies a
common American-Arab strategy on the oil
question, but makes a united American-Israeli
one most realistic. The key operational factors
are nonetheless military in character: Israel has
the aerial reach to appear in the Persian Gulf and
make her military presence felt. There were indi-
cations in the recent past that the U.S. air force

had been using Israel's air base at Etzion in the southern Sinai for long-range surveillance flights over the Gulf of Aden and the western areas of the Indian Ocean. This is not incompatible with an actual deployment of Israeli forces for emergency combat in the Persian Gulf. Whatever the specific formula, some kind of American-Israeli coordination to assure the free flow of oil to the West could be worked out. Former Senator Frank Church called for a credible American step to indicate to the Soviet Union that the US will defend the oil fields if that should become necessary. He suggested an American agreement with Israel for base rights to demonstrate Washington's determination on this matter. Israel, looking anxiously southward to the growing Saudi military buildup at Tabuk and herself in distress over energy losses due to the Sinai withdrawal, would be a natural ally of America if both countries felt compelled to act in the Persian Gulf zone.

The Mediterranean Ocean

The security of the eastern Mediterranean basin is vital for the strength of NATO's southern flank against Soviet threats. The role of Turkey as part of the Western alignment in this zone is at best problematic today. Violence and religious instability are weakening its internal balance; it is, from an external point of view, somewhat alienated from the Western world's major concerns since the use by the Islamic-Arab world of oil as a weapon against Europe. The considerable Russian naval buildup in the Mediterranean has yet to be met by a viable American response. If Israel was to receive a sufficient number of F-15 and F-16 planes, the most sophisticated fighters in the world, General Keegan maintains that Israel — employing a fleet of ten tankers at sea — could control USSR aggressive intrusion in the eastern Mediterranean.[28] At the least Israel — and probably only Israel — could provide secure air cover for the US Sixth Fleet. It is worth emphasizing that according to widespread professional military judgment the Israeli air force is one of the best, if not *the best*, in the world. And F-15s in Israeli hands will not suddenly fall into Soviet hands —what is certainly not true for F-15s in Saudi hands.

The Horn of Africa
   Western fortunes are sliding in the African Horn particularly since Ethiopia developed tight ties with the Russians and eliminated American use of the Kagnew communications station. Cuban troops have served as a proxy Soviet force to help Ethiopia keep Somalia at bay; yet Somalia, which formerly expelled the Russians, may now want to renew links with them. All this makes the USSR the key power in the Horn, where America's weakness and restraint have won no victories and have dismayed many friends (like

the Saudis). Israel, which like the United States also had close ties with Ethiopia, is very concerned about the Horn area and its proximity to the Bab el-Mandab entrance to the Red Sea that leads up to Eilat, Israel's southern port in the Gulf of Aqaba. The dramatic raid to Entebbe, Uganda in 1976 demonstrated the long arm of Israeli aerial power deep into Africa. This is just one instance of Israel's national resolve to defend its basic interests whenever this is at all possible. A similar American determination can perhaps prevent the Horn of Africa from falling altogether into the Soviet sphere.

4) A Rational Alliance

Israel sits at the axis point of three major theaters of action in regional and global terms: she is pivoted eastward to the Persian Gulf, westward to the Mediterranean Ocean, and southward to the African Horn. Her military capacity and political reliability can help transform American power in the Middle East from a formal declaration to an active force. It is no doubt with such thoughts in mind that analysts like Ray Cline, Eugene Rostow, and others identify Israel — but no Arab-Muslim state — as an important member of a viable and sturdy American-led Western alliance system. Or to quote from the Generals' letter:

> ...the ability of the U.S. to protect its security interests in the Middle East is

closely linked, if not dependent on, the maintenance of a potent Israeli military capability in the area.

In this context, a U.S. Interagency study on the global military balance concluded recently that, in the event of a non-nuclear superpower conflict in the Middle East, Israel, by itself, 'might deter Soviet combat forces' intervention or prevent the completion of such deployment'. At this stage, no other society in the area can be counted on to mobilize reliable, battle-tested ground and air units, or to make available secure access points. In brief, if not for the proven capability of the Israeli armed forces, we would be forced now to station a significant number of men and substantial materiel in that region.

This is one of the strongest statements acclaiming Israel as a paramount American *interest*: she no longer simply benefits from Washington's *commitment* to her welfare but, rather, contributes significantly to the welfare of the United States and Western strategic interests in the Middle East. It remains to be seen to what degree Israel will be asked, or allowed, to shore up Washington's interest in the future.

In order for Israel to assume a major responsibility as a strategic ally she must be as militarily strong as possible. One fundamental component of such strength will be her territorial dimensions which, since the peace process began, are diminishing in Sinai and perhaps in other areas in the near future. Such a constricted, vulnerable country is unfit to serve as a 'regional power' — Israel's future role in the words of the Atlantic Council. A state with no strategic depth, a width of just *10 miles*, suffering from topographical disadvantages in the east and north, lacking oil resources, without national confidence and social dynamism — such a country will not be fit to be anything resembling a 'regional power'. Therefore, the American peace formula for a restricted Israel in the narrow pre-1967 lines inevitably eliminates the possibility of America enjoying the advantages of an Israeli power linked to US strategic efforts in the Middle East. The formula also creates the conditions for the eventual establishment of a PLO state, supported by the USSR, in the West Bank and the Gaza Strip. Sadat may have expelled the Russians in 1972, but America seems intent on inviting them back into the area.

The abuse of Israel, rather than her use, is inherent in Washington's effort to push Israel out of Judea and Samaria/West Bank. This territory is 2000 square miles, the size of Delaware for example. From a military point of view its value to Israel is obvious: if lost to Israel the country is purely indefensible as Arab forces, sitting on the mountain ranges overlooking the exposed coastal strip around Tel Aviv, could cut the country in two in a swift tank thrust through the lowlands to the sea just 10 miles wide.[29] Abba Eban's phrase certainly hits the mark: the 1967 lines are the borders of Auschwitz. No peace formula or security provision can alter that stark reality.

The American view of Israeli-Arab peace has accepted some of Israel's procedural demands and most of the Arabs' substantive demands. Washington favors direct negotiations between the parties, but yet supports the Arab position of an Israeli withdrawal from all the territories. (The notion of 'cosmetic border changes' implies nothing more than moving the line a few hundred meters, and even then maybe in mutual boundary alterations by both sides.) This indicates that both America and the Arab states together seek to push Israel back to the indefensible former borders. The US is willing to leave the Panama Canal only in the year 2000 and even then retain the right to return there if necessary, notwithstanding that it is not critical to American national security and some 2000 miles from Washington. However, Israel is expected to withdraw from Judea and Samaria in five years at the latest from the 1979 signing of the Camp David Treaty, notwithstanding that the territory sits in the heart of Israel and the likely Arab ruler will be the Soviet-supported PLO determined to continue its struggle from a position surrounding

Jerusalem on all sides and overlooking the Jewish population concentration on the coastal plain below. The most ardent American defenders of the Panama treaty are unwilling to base their country's security on faith and trust. But Israel is called upon to place the welfare of its four million inhabitants and the very survival of its national existence on a chance roll of the dice.[30]

Much of America's hope for peace rested on the credibility of President Sadat of Egypt. He dramatically began a dialogue with Israel that has changed the face of the Middle East. However much one legitimately recognizes that most positive step, it would be well to remember that Sadat, like 'rejectionist' Arab leaders, continued to demand a peace settlement — the 1967 borders and 'Palestinian rights' — that will leave Israel literally gasping for breath. In March 1980 he outlined the Egyptian national vision in a working paper called "Egypt and The New Arab Reality". In it Sadat revealed, though not for the first time, the difference between his policy towards Israel and that of other Arab states:

> Despite the present differences with the Arab 'rejectionist' rulers over the Egyptian peace initiative the fact remains that those differences are only tactical not strategic, temporary not permanent.[31]

There is in this statement a clear hint that Sadat shared with other Arabs the view that Israel is an illegitimate entity in the heart of the Arab nation that must eventually disappear — by war or peace, combat or diplomacy.

No state should rely for its national well-being on promises of good will or commitments based on past friendship. Israel has no alternative but to rely on her own capacity to protect her vital interests with all the national confidence and military strength, moral assuredness and legal legitimacy, that she can conjure up at this dangerous time of her history. Israel's ability to maintain a viable national existence is a precondition to be a 'regional power' that can contribute to the American-led Western strategic alignment in the Middle East today.

We may now end this analysis by briefly summarizing how America can achieve its basic national goals in the region by adopting a close alliance posture with Israel. From appearing as an unwelcome burden Israel now looks like a welcome blessing. The following points are relevant regarding the three fundamental US interests:

1) The Arab-Israeli Conflict

America seeks to realize peace and prevent war in the context of the Arab-Israeli conflict. A weakened Israel, lacking territorial depth and possibly denied weapons from Washington, will be unable to employ a credible deterrent posture to prevent the Arabs from considering a war option. Any semblance of an 'abandoned Israel' will diminish the chances of peace which are always enhanced when Israel is perceived as strong rather than weak. In fact, the image of a tough and powerful Israel may have induced Sadat to adopt the path of negotiations in 1977. But it is fundamentally a strategically viable Israel that can deter war and create the conditions for peace.

In addition, continued American support for Israel is vital to assure the general credibility of US foreign commitments. On this point Elmo Zumwalt, Jr., former chief of naval operations, has said:

> The first thing that would happen in the event of a decision by the United States to throw Israel out of the sled to the wolves would be, in my judgment, the destruction of any remaining value of our alliances anywhere around the world.[32]

After Vietnam, Taiwan, Iran, Lebanon, and others, the abandonment of Israel would raise grave fears among America's West European allies that they are next in line. Without intention 'Fortress America' would find itself, sooner or later, abandoned in the world facing foes with no friends by its side.

2) The Soviet Threat

Only Israel, of all Middle East countries, has

the will and capacity to actively deter further Russian penetration of the region. Alone, it would be a most difficult task. If joined by moderate Arab regimes linking their future to the United States, Israel could lead a powerful bloc of nations against the Soviet-supported group. In spite of the conflict between Arabs and Israel both sides are equally threatened by the imperial designs of Moscow. According to a recent report the USSR is experiencing a decline in its oil production and will require Persian Gulf oil by approximately the late 1980's.[33] Developments in Afghanistan, Iran, and elsewhere suggest the Russians may not wait that long. Now is the time to form a joint Israeli-Arab effort, supported by America, to defend the independence of small nations against the Soviet threat. There is no sign that Arab states on their own, individually or even collectively, have the will and capacity to deter the Russians. Israel, based on its past record along the Suez Canal, in Lebanon, and vis-à-vis Syria, can help turn Soviet adventurism into a foolhardy policy.

3) The Oil Threat

The oil problem will continue to haunt the Western world until America produces a credible deterrent posture against the Arab oil-producing countries. The Free World cannot be subject to a 'global tea tax' that saps its inner strength and external stature. With Israel, and perhaps other nations, the United States can begin to assure the smooth shipment of oil; it is important in this regard that the dismal failure of the operation to free the American hostages in Iran in late April 1980 not deter Washington from acting in the region of the Persian Gulf in the future when necessary. Israel can help make such an American commitment a credible strategic stance.

We may conclude that what weakens Israel also weakens America, and vice versa. America and Israel, acting together, can make possible a true Arab-Israeli peace, block the path to further Russian expansionism, and try and assure the flow of oil to the West. An American-Israeli strategic relationship is based on principle and pragmatism, joining consideration for a moral posture with a Realpolitik outlook. In this way America could make a major effort toward realizing regional stability and protecting fundamental Western interests in the Middle East. 'When bad men combine', said Edmund Burke, 'the good must associate; else they will fall one by one, an unpitied sacrifice in a contemptible struggle.'

Before Columbus set sail for America, he had dreamt of the Far East, and of the round world, and of the trackless ocean. Adventure rarely reaches its predetermined end. Columbus never reached China. But he discovered America.

Alfred North Whitehead,
Adventures of Ideas, ch. XIX

CHAPTER 4:

AN AFTERWORD ON NATIONAL CHARACTER

The political behavior of a state is determined considerably by the cultural norms of the society. The cultural fabric of a society is the substructure that forms the basis for political ideas, institutions, and actions that constitute the superstructure in the social universe of a nation. It follows that if America does not understand the culture of Arab-Muslim societies then it shall fail to comprehend, let alone predict, their politics. It also follows that if the argument that was advanced demands a change of US policy towards the Mideast, then that new political orientation may be possible only if there is a cultural adaption in America itself. If the Arabs will not, or cannot, act very different from the way they act today because of the sturdy and static cultural underpinnings in their societies, it is reasonable to claim as well that the Americans cannot act different politically than the way they have been acting unless they alter their cultural habits. Peoples usually do not quickly change their basic national feelings and patterns of behavior.

The feasibility of a close American-Israeli alignment, which entails a considerable shift in Washington policy-making, will depend on a reevaluation in national self-perception for both the United States and Israel. This implies that the cultural substructure is rather 'thick-skinned' forcing its enveloping presence upon the political superstructure. For the sake of clarity and specification it will be helpful to identify two areas where cultural alterations are needed.

The traditionally dominant American policy conception on the Middle East is largely tied to the realization of immediate satisfactions. As a society America is always on the move, gesticulating frantically with new ideas and fads, never clinging to old forms. This national characteristic was perceptively analyzed by Alexis de Tocqueville 150 years ago in his classic study on *Democracy in America*:

> It is strange to see with what feverish ardour the Americans pursue their own welfare; and to watch the vague dread that constantly torments them lest they should

> not have chosen the shortest path which
> may lead to it...
> In the United States a man builds a house
> to spend his latter years in it, and he sells it
> before the roof is on: he plants a garden,
> and lets it just as the trees are coming into
> bearing; he brings a field into tillage, and
> leaves other men to gather the crops; he
> embraces a profession and gives it up; he
> settles in a place, which he soon after-
> wards leaves...[1]

This interminable nervous agitation and rest-
lessness prevent any long-term planning of affairs by Americans. They change their mind as
often as other people change their clothes.

There is often a feeling of national emergency
and grave urgency in US policy-making on the
Mideast: the Arab-Israeli conflict must be resolved immediately, for example, even though a
close examination reveals that the conditions for
peace are hardly at hand. The American approach is to submit to Arab oil blackmail rather
than concentrate all national efforts on developing alternative energy sources. The Russian advance must be halted right away, though a more
credible response is the concerted buildup over
time of a credible American force to deter Soviet
expansionism. The key word is *Now:* from instant coffee to instant political solutions in a culture which demands, in its habitual optimism,

the elimination of all evil, sickness, and tragedy with one wave of the wand.

A mature American posture would seek to cultivate national values of commitment, patience, and perseverance. There are no shortcuts to resolve major problems, but only hard thinking and hard work. Often, the fruits of serious labor are not quickly picked; the most valuable prizes come after extended and difficult effort. This is a realistic outlook when America considers the problems it faces in the Mideast. The administration's erratic behavior regarding American hostages in Iran — alternating from diplomatic negotiations to servile submission to the use of violence itself — is symptomatic of the vacillating character of US policy-making. Washington must match Moscow's long-range planning perspective with one of its own. To work closely with Israel is most decidedly *not* to expect rapid success in any major foreign policy endeavor. This is building from the ground up in setting the foundations for a sturdy structure of strategic cooperation.

In working with the unstable Arab world there is hardly a basis for long-range planning; here Washington rests its policy on the hope that the present freezes into the future. Yet that is an unfounded wish, not a reasoned judgment. But America can *plan* with Israel a future that can be an improvement on the present assuming it is

willing to delay immediate gratification of its de-
sires.

The second area of cultural change required in
America concerns the relations between Jews
and non-Jews. As a country with a deep Christian heritage, folklore, and belief-system, the
United States cannot help but have absorbed
something of the negative disposition towards
the Jewish people as borne through the ages. The
Christian world, or large segments of it, has de-
picted the Jew as a weak, despicable, unattrac-
tive figure destined to be a social outcast and a
cultural inferior. On no account was he to control his own life and be independent of the
world's control or free of its wrath.

Israel today — and certainly the Israel depict-
ed in the argument for a strategic relationship
with America — is a powerful nation with military capacity to defend itself, and much more. It
is able to flex its muscles and walk with a straight
back. It claims rights for itself and can often
achieve them through its own power. This new
Jewish reality can be hard for Christians to swal-
low who, while witnessing the persecution of
Jews in the past, were overwhelmed and im-
pressed by their capacity for merciful, eloquent,
and gentle behavior in spite of it all. Now the
Jew — the Israeli — wants to do all he can, with
the means he possesses that Jews in worse circumstances did not possess, to assure his physical welfare. Daniel Berrigan was most discom-

forted when the Jews arose from the Holocaust 'like warriors, armed to the teeth'.[2] He would have preferred that either they not arise, or arise as ghostly shadows, spiritual entities, pure and pacific: but not as a normal people seeking natural national existence in its own land, utilizing the necessary methods of state-building in the international arena.

No doubt a residual element of this rejection of the physical Jew with power in his hands influences the American preference for an alliance with Arab states, rather than with Israel. Washington will have to alter its cultural portrait of the Jew, not only its political policy towards Israel. And without the former the latter may be an impossibility.

For Israel we should like to identify two parallel cultural aspects that require alteration to make an alignment with America a real option. Like American society, and because it too is a Western country in many respects, the preoccupation with immediate gratification is widespread in Israel. People seek ease and relaxation wherever possible, particularly since much of Israeli life is marred with economic difficulty and military tensions. For over thirty years Israelis have hoped for a solution to the conflict with the Arabs. Typically, in Western cultural terms, the cry went out for Peace *Now*. Tomorrow is another day and they would prefer worrying about it when they get there, assuming of course they get there.

Consistent with this social pattern, Israeli policy-making has not been characterized by long-term planning. The country has often seemed to hope for peace as a solution to fundamental dangers and weaknesses rather than responsibly mapping out a national strategy for Israeli survival. The latter approach would call for great national effort and sacrifice; the puristic peace approach calls for nothing more than a belief in an Arab change of attitude towards Israel. One path calls for struggle and persistence, the other for good fortune and something resembling appeasing the Arab world, if not capitulating to its demands. Israel has lacked the courage, strength, and vision to plan an independent alternative course for long-term national welfare and self-sufficiency.

As a potentially vital partner with America in the Middle East, Israel will need to adopt an attitude that looks beyond the requirements of today. It must lay the foundations for a country that knows where it wants to go and what it needs to get there. Only with a clear sense now of what Israel will look like in the upcoming decades — in terms of military might, territorial size, and social fabric — can America enter into a tight relationship with her. Washington has a right to know what Israel promises to be as they enter into a long-term pact.

As America contends with adjusting its image of the Jew, Israel too must define, or re-define, its own perception it has of itself. The Jew has cultivated a spiritual sense of who he is, often transforming literal definitions of physical strength into spiritual categories.[3] This traditional religious commentary has colored Jewish culture over the centuries and was partially maintained even in the radical departure signalled by the Zionist revolution in the modern era. In this latter context the Jew came to the Land of Israel to 'build the land and build himself', to conquer nature but not to rule the Arab population. Just as the Rabbinic sages turned Joshua and King David into scholars and poets, so the modern-day Israeli commentators would turn Ben-Gurion into a philosophic muse and Dayan into an archeological dreamer. Spiritual concerns would be more authentic and legitimate than the physical dimension of life.

Israel and its Jews must come to terms — comfortably and unashamedly — with the military character of their national existence. This was certainly not part of the Zionist vision but it has sadly become inseparable from Middle Eastern reality. The army is an Israeli way of life and warfare has been imposed by the Arabs on the Jews' social diet. Israel's impressive combat successes should be accepted for what they are, not hidden in the drawer while Jaffa oranges and womens' dress fashions are paraded in front of the world. When Israel will fully and finally accept that its physical reality has a powerful mil-

itary face to it, then its own self-image as a Jewish state will appropriately adapt to this. Its
Jewishness will not be impaired by this realization. Ultimately, it is equally the material as well
as the spiritual essence of Israel that earns the
world's admiration. That point should be recognized as Israel seeks a strategic relationship with
the United States.

America and Israel represent the 'chosen' societies that carry the most noble dreams of civilization. If they shall prosper and be strong, the
Western world may be able to avoid a nightmar-
ish threat being conspired in other quarters. Together they can even turn an *alliance* into a *covenant* and assure that their links are deeper even
than the basic political interests that bind them.
This may rest on the Biblical promise referring to
the world's orientation towards the Jewish people. The divine declaration to Abraham and his
people was: "I shall bless those that bless thee
and curse those that curse thee, and in you shall
all the peoples of the earth be blessed."[4] And so
must America choose its policy in the Middle
East.

There is no doubt that one convenant established some 3700 years ago will always remain
the national bedrock of Jewish destiny. This is
the covenant that the Jewish people made with
the Land of Israel through the medium of the
God of History. America's own national origins
200 years ago were rooted in the spirit of conve-

nant ideology and that creates a natural meeting ground for the two peoples. Israel, the Lion of Judah reawakened, will undoubtedly strive to realize the hopes of generations of Jews in the modern era even if this must be done in adversity against powerful enemies and alone. This Israeli determination should never be in doubt and America, the Great Eagle, should realize this fact and prove herself worthy of the covenant.

———————

I wrote to the Pope and never got an answer. He is supposed to be our spiritual father on the ground, and each father is supposed to protect his son, even if he is wrong. The terrorists are getting volunteers from Iran, Libya, Iraq, Saudi Arabia, from all the Communist countries, to fight for them. What prevents the Christians from sending funds or coming as volunteers to help us? We feel left out from all the world except by Israel. We are fortunate that we found Israel on our border to help us. Israel understood our problem, that we are a minority threatened with extermination, and extended its hand to us.

Major Saad Haddad, Maronite head of Southern Lebanon *The New York Times*, May 19, 1980.

APPENDIX

THE 1982 WAR IN LEBANON

On June 5, 1982 — exactly fifteen years after the 1967 Six Day War — the Israeli army carried out a major punitive and pre-emptive invasion of Lebanon to destroy the military power of the PLO in that distraught country. For a decade the PLO established a mini-Palestinian entity within the southern and central parts of Lebanon, destroying its delicate communal balance and political integrity, and installing a 'Reign of Terror' that eliminated any semblance of law and order, peace and security, in the Land of the Cedars. Only in the wake of Israel's incursion did the most grotesque atrocities of the PLO's presence became known. They include the rape of Christian women, the militarization of all civilian life, the ruin of urban commerce, the mobilization of 12-year-old youth into terrorist gangs, and the

practise of vandalism as a way of life. The Pales-
tinization of Lebanon in the 1970s resulted from
the PLO occupation force: returning Lebanon to
the Lebanese in the 1980s might be the major
achievement from the Israeli Liberating force
that smashed the PLO's military might.

On June 2, 1982 the Lebanese newspaper *Al-
Nahar* reported that 2,379 people had been killed
and 6,518 had been wounded in Lebanon during
1981. The overwhelming number of casualties
were in Beirut which is an urban battleground
for over 100 militias that control the city and
wreck murder and destruction. The ideological
conflicts of the entire Arab world play themselves out violently in Lebanon; the Syrians fight
the Iraqis, the Iraqis the Iranians, while a multitude of Palestinian factions, Nasserites, Moslem
Brotherhood forces, Armenians, Kurds, Alawis,
and tens of other organizations prevent the paci-
fication and unification of Lebanon. Residential
areas became armed bases, refugee camps became military strongholds, every house in West
Beirut had a mortar or heavy machine gun. In
his penetrating book called *The Arab Predicament* (p. 4), Fouad Ajami captured the grimness
and tragedy of the situation:

> The young thugs roaming the streets of
> Beirut and the snipers on its tall and
> modern buildings that once stood as a
> monument to Lebanon's 'cosmopolitan-

ism' exposed the tribalism of a deeply
sectarian country whose civilized forms
were only a cover for biases and prejudices, an escape from realities intuited and
known by its inhabitants.

The new found wealth and power of the Arab
world could not prevent the most sophisticated
of Arab cities from being drenched in this irre-
versible blood bath. Close to 100,000 Lebanese
have lost their lives since the outbreak of the
Civil War in April, 1975.

The massive destruction in Lebanon reflected
inter-Arab struggles and PLO violence that had
little relationship to the Arab-Israeli conflict.
The terrorist movement set up bases in the
southern part of the country, along the coast in
Tyre and Sidon, at Nabatiya and in Fatahland
towards the east. This led to the migration of
some 300,000 Shiite Muslims to Beirut, but yet
aroused the determination of Maronite elements,
led by Major Saad Haddad, to assert their rights
to their land by forging with Israel's assistance
an autonomous fighting force of their own. Indeed, Haddad proclaimed the political entity of a
"Free Lebanon" in the south in April, 1979.

Entrenched on Lebanese soil since the early
1970s, the PLO carried out a policy of shelling
Israeli civilian settlements in the northern Galilee and sending in terrorist bands, by land and
sea, to murder Jews wherever they could be

found. The names Maalot, Shamir, Kiryat Shmona, Nahariya and Misgav Am are reminders of PLO terrorism and its bloody history in Israel. A life of fear was the permanent reality for Israelis in the Galilee; growing up in bomb shelters was the environment for Israeli children during the day and night. The Litani Operation of 1978 achieved certain positive results for Israel but the border could not be hermetically sealed, the United Nations force (UNIFIL) became a mere symbol of international impotency, and terror continued to stalk the country. The last straw was the PLO attempted assassination of Israel's ambassador in London, Shlomo Argov. The Israeli government under prime minister Begin decided on a strategic incursion into Lebanon — *not against Lebanon* — to destroy PLO military forces and infrastructure throughout southern Lebanon and their headquarters in Beirut.

The war that began in June, 1982 was an eye-opener in a number of ways. The Israel Defense Forces (IDF) uncovered enough light arms, ammunition, and ancillary weapons in PLO bunkers to equip five infantry brigades. PLO military stores, often built into mountain ridges and stretching for over 100 yards in length, included weapons from the Soviet Union, North Korea, China and war material from Western countries. The enormous amounts suggested PLO plans for a long military struggle against

Israel, much wider in scope than had been
known until 1982.

Israel's impressive advance northward set the
PLO fleeing and led to the capture of some 5,000
terrorists by the IDF. It was this development
which liberated the Lebanese — Christians and
Muslims — from PLO occupation. The large
Shiite population, spearheaded by their militia
El-Amal, began to more openly oppose the PLO
and took steps to cooperate with Haddad's army
in the south. The Lebanese were ecstatic and ge-
nuinely appreciative that Israel had, in fulfilling
its national interests, also liberated them as well.
An immense sense of relief was felt. It was manifested in the massive move by Lebanese civilians
southward, back to the homes they had abandoned when the PLO had establised its reign of
terror a few years earlier.

Another fascinating eye-opener therefore concerned the Lebanese reaction to the destruction
wrought by Israel's military operations against
the PLO. Honest observers of the political scene
always knew that the PLO had often established
military bases in civilian areas. For example, the
Ain el-Hilweh refugee camp in Sidon was a PLO
center and this practise of hiding behind women
and children was certainly one of the more in-
human and cruel methods in terrorist mobilization and warfare. As a result, civilian destruction
became an unavoidable part of Israel's warfare
against the PLO. However, and this is the eye-

opener, Lebanese civilians accepted their own
suffering as innocent victims of the conflict with
a deep feeling of satisfaction. United States Congressman Charles Wilson visited the country and
had the following impression to report (Israeli
radio, June 26, 1982):

> I stopped at Sidon where, as you know,
> the damage was severe... and in talking
> to a group of people, some of whom had
> lost relatives — they said it was awful,
> but they said that, all in all, to be free of
> the PLO, it was worth it —and that was a
> profound realization to me. I intend to
> try to get the word out at home that the
> citizens — the Lebanese themselves —
> are glad it happened.

Congressman Wilson was truly astonished that
the Lebanese received the Israelis as liberators,
but whoever knew the truth about the PLO's
presence in Lebanon for the last decade was not
really surprised. The paradoxes of Middle East
political life brought together an interesting alliance between the Jews and the Christians, the
Israelis and the Lebanese, both seeking peace
and stability in their respective homelands. The
PLO was their common enemy.

At this point it is instructive to turn to the
wider political and strategic implications from
the war in Lebanon. American policy towards

the June-July events failed to crystallize and reflected a befuddling confusion about which side
to support, when, and to what degree. The sud-
den resignation of Secretary of State Alexander
Haig and his replacement by George Shultz indicated the confusion in Washington and the interminable tensions in policy-making regarding
the Middle East. At least in part, Haig's exit sig-
nified his failure to alter the pro-Arab policy paradigm in favor of a more balanced equilibrium
that would have recognized Israel as a formidable strategic asset to the United States. He tried
unsuccessfully to turn the corner in US foreign
policy. The war in Lebanon created possibilities
for American strategic innovation that went un-
exploited by the Reagan administration.

Israel's initial military victories in Lebanon
against the PLO and the Syrian army inflicted a
damaging blow to the Soviet alliance system in
the Arab world. With Iraq suffering in the gulf
war from Iranian military momentum, the plight
of Syria losing 101 planes in dogfights against
the Israeli air force and the destruction of SA6,
SA8, and SA9 missile batteries in the Bekaa Val-
ley cost the Russians a major loss in strategic
stature in the 'northern tier' of the Arab world.
The weakening of the PLO eliminates, perhaps
permanently, a major instrument of international terrorism that the communist world has utilized against the West with devastating damage
to the integrity of liberal societies.

The defeat of Soviet-bloc satellites, Syria and the PLO, enhances the strategic value of all American-oriented Arab countries like Egypt and Saudi Arabia. The patriotic Lebanese forces tend naturally to identify with the Western world for historical, religious, and political reasons, and see the struggle for Lebanon as a struggle of the West itself. Bashir Gemayel, the head of the Phalangist forces, explained the unique opportunity at hand with the PLO-Syrian losses. In an interview on ABC-TV on June 27, 1982 Gemayel called for the establishment of 'a new political regime for both Christians and Moslems... a real modern state, democratic, liberal state... parliamentary system... We are going to start building up this country'. This is clearly the language of Western politics and not communist totalitarianism. He hopes the West will assume its moral duty to the Christians of Lebanon. All of these things have now become possible in the interests of the Western world due to Israel's impressive legitimate war of defense in Lebanon.

The setback to the Arab Rejectionist Front from the Lebanese War might entail a dramatic readjustment of power and national purpose in the Arab world. The so-called "moderate" regimes in Egypt and Saudi Arabia proved politically inept to the same degree that the "radical" regimes in Syria, Iraq, and the PLO itself proved militarily inept. The Saudis, touted as major defenders of the Palestinian movement, were moved to beseech the United States to intervene to save the PLO in Western Beirut while they stood by, due to choice or circumstance. The ideological Palestinian glue meant to cement the Arab nation behind the struggle against Israel did not hold together. Indeed, the awful soul-searching that reverberated throughout the Arab world following the June loss in 1967 might be repeated following the Lebanese War in 1982 as the Arabs ask what went wrong: what about Arab unity? what about the Palestinian cause? what about Arab power? All Arab factors showed themselves ineffective in one way or another and it will be intriguing to see how the Arab world reorganizes its forces and decides upon its future course of action. There is no doubt that much of the Arab world was secretly and ironically pleased to see the PLO so devastatingly overrun by Israel. The PLO has proven to be a nuisance and a threat to more than one Arab state over the years, even though its ideological and political value is central to the concerted Arab campaign against Israel.

It was to be hoped that America might prove itself capable of exploiting this new situation to strengthen its interests in the Mideast. Yet Washington seemed intent, perhaps not too surprisingly, to keep kicking itself in the face. The pro-Soviet PLO was on the verge of total defeat, but America was determined not only to save it but to cultivate a sort of political dialogue with it.

Israel was smashing the Syrian pro-Soviet ally, though American officials trivialized the matter by criticizing the use by Israel of American weapons in doing so. The US administration was outraged by the phenomenon of civilian suffering caused by Israeli warfare, yet overlooked the fact that the PLO had installed a terrorist regime against the Lebanese population for some seven years, and the fact that the Lebanese greeted the Israeli force as a liberating army.

The Arab world had abandoned the PLO to Hussein's army in Amman in 1970, to Assad's army in Tel el-Zaatar in 1976, and once again to Israel's army in Beirut, in 1982. But none other than America tried to come to the PLO's rescue against Israel. This episode touched on the agony of Israel's permanent predicament in its relations with America.

American policy did admittedly show some balance and indicated an understanding for Israeli positions. The US delegation at the United Nations Security Council vetoed a resolution calling for an immediate Israeli withdrawal from the area of Beirut, and Washington supported Jerusalem's call for an end to all foreign presence in Lebanon (i.e., Syrian and PLO). Nonetheless, the inescapable overall impression remained that the Reagan team showed a lack of vigorous leadership and was unable to articulate a coherent policy on the war. From the perspective of US-defined national interests, nothing but self-defeating contradiction plagued America's efforts throughout this period.

The conjunction of American-Israeli interests in the 1982 Lebanese War can be summarized as follows:

1. Weakening of Soviet power and prestige in the Arab world;
2. Weakening of radical anti-Western Arab countries and the PLO;
3. Strengthening of US diplomatic maneuverability among moderate Arab countries;
4. Strengthening of Western-oriented Lebanon as a national entity free of foreign intervention;
5. Gathering intelligence information on various sophisticated Soviet weaponry, such as the T-72 tank, and the demonstration of Israel's technological edge in electronic and aerial warfare in destroying the most advanced Soviet missile batteries;
6. Developing naval possibilities in the eastern Mediterranean basin based on the restraint of the Soviet navy and the ineffectiveness of the Syrian navy during the war.

Although it would be hazardous to draw firm conclusions from this most recent war, taking place as it is in a volatile Middle East, two pertinent thoughts should be stated: that a new strategic balance is emerging in the region that rests on Israel's preeminence and that, as a consequence, the American-Israeli relationship in concert with some realistic Arab regimes may be able to creatively use the new situation to solidify the peace process in the Middle East.

America still requires much courage and self-critical conviction to free itself of former conceptions and utilize the event of the Lebanese war for articulating a new constructive regional policy. Any propagandistic jargon referring to the PLO as a 'national liberation movement' will not only alienate Israel and confound certain Arab 'moderates', but will ultimately strengthen a Soviet satellite against US interests. Any American-PLO dialogue will lower the moral stature of America as a nation because the PLO itself is no more worthy of recognition than Baader-Meinhof or the Red Brigades and, after Israel's resounding military show-of-force, no more critical a political factor in the Middle East than those two gangs are in Western Europe. Any American criticism of the alleged immorality of the war conducted by Israel is also a dubious, hypocritical charge. Those voices in America that argue for linking US foreign assistance to the moral quality of the recipient party must logically abandon any idea of supporting the PLO — whose record on the question of civil rights is as dismal as they come and more barbaric than most. Ask the Lebanese.

Any American attack on the Begin government in Israel charging that it distorts the popular will and carries out a major policy against the views of a majority of Israelis is pure falsehood. Aside from marginal expressions of opposition to "The War for Peace in the Galilee", the overwhelming feeling in the country was supportive. One opinion poll in late June asked who the respondent would vote for if an election was then held: the results indicated that Begin's Likud Party would be returned to office with 59 seats when they then had only 46! Another poll found 83 percent of Israelis in favor of the government's conduct of the war. It is a gross and persistent distortion of the truth to claim that Menachem Begin rides roughshod over the will of the Israeli people. He governs the country with the strong support of a democratic majority.

The 1982 war in Lebanon provided the most recent evidence for the identity of American and Israeli interests on global and regional issues, as the evolution of a new balance of power in the Middle East suggested the practicality of realizing them. This political thesis may seem unexotic for some Americans searching for a grand Oriental enterprise, but it is such a solid strategy that the pragmatism of the American Experiment can continue to avoid it only at its own national expense. It will be unfortunate if the United States irresponsibly misses another opportunity to incorporate the Israeli asset into its permanent foreign policy conception towards the region. Missed opportunities do not always return.

NOTES

CHAPTER 1

[1] From Graham D. Vernon, "Controlled Conflict: Soviet Perceptions of Peaceful Coexistence," *Orbis,* Summer 1979, p. 283n29. Brezhnev has referred to 'the last decisive battle, the battle for the overthrow of capitalism' that he anticipates in the near future. America is for him the last bastion of capitalism that must be overthrown.

[2] Raymond L. Garthoff, "Soviet Views on the Interrelation of Diplomacy and Military Strategy," *Political Science Quarterly,* Fall 1979, pp. 391-405. See also Fritz W. Ermarth, "Contrasts in American and Soviet Strategic Thought," *International Security,* Fall 1978, pp. 139-49.

[3] 'The World According to Brzezinski', *The New York Times Magazine,* December 31, 1978, p. 11.

[4] *U.S. News and World Report,* Jan. 7, 1980, p. 38.

[5] Edward T. Hall, *The Hidden Dimension* (Garden City, N.Y.: Doubleday, 1966), p. 144. For an interesting cultural portrait of Arabs for Western readers, see Raphael Patai, *The Arab Mind* (New York: Charles Scribner's Sons, 1976).

[6] *Middle East Peace Prospects, Hearings before the Subcommittee on Near Eastern and South Asian Affairs of the Committee on Foreign Relations,* U.S. Senate, 94th Congress, July 26, 1976 (Washington: U.S. Govt. Printing Office, 1976), p. 351.

[7] For a close analysis of Arab formulations to express the goal of Israel's destruction, see Y. Harkabi, *Arab Attitudes to Israel* (Jerusalem: Keter, 1976), esp. ch. 1.

[8] Anwar el-Sadat, *In Search of Identity: An Autobio-*

graphy (New York: Harper & Row, 1978), p. 244. Interesting approaches to capture Sadat's true character are found in Paul Eidelberg, *Sadat's Strategy* (Montreal: Dawn Pub., 1979) and by Gail Sheehy, "The Riddle of Sadat," *Esquire,* Jan. 30, 1979, pp. 25-39.

[9] Jesse W. Lewis, Jr., *The Strategic Balance in the Mediterranean* (Washington: American Enterprise Institute for Public Policy Research, 1976), p. 110.

[10] *Le Monde,* 25-26 Sept. 1977.

[11] *Iran: Evaluation of U.S. Intelligence Performance Prior To November 1978, Permanent Select Committee on Intelligence,* U.S. House of Representatives, Jan. 1979 (Washington: Govt. Printing Office, 1979), p. 2.

[12] Resolution 242 contains a controversial article which similarly seems to deny any Israeli claim to territorial retention. It calls for 'withdrawal of Israeli armed forces from territories occupied in the recent conflict'. The absence of the preposition "all" preceding "territories" has not inhibited Arab spokesmen from demanding a complete Israeli pullback *from all* the territories. And the inference that territories "occupied in the recent conflict" must be withdrawn has not inhibited Israel from claiming that there is no explicit obligation to, in fact, pull back *from all* the territories.

[13] Alfred L. Atherton, Jr., "The Middle East Peace Process: A Status Report," Los Angeles, June 15, 1978.

[14] In ideological terms Israel and Palestine are mutually exclusive terms and the attempt to politically apply them makes any compromise near impossible. On this point, Mordechai Nisan, "The Israeli-Palestine Antithesis," *The Jerusalem Post,* Feb. 3, 1980.

[15] Paul Johnson, *The Seven Deadly Sins of Terrorism,* The Jonathan Institute (Jerusalem), 1979.

[16] Jack F. Kemp, "The Soviet Threat," *AEI Defense Review,* II, 3, p. 15.

[17] Prepared Statement of Major-General George J. Keegan, Jr., USAF (ret.), *The Subcommittee on Near Eastern and South Asian Affairs,* U.S. Senate Committee on Foreign Relations, October 3, 1977 (Washington: Govt. Printing Office, 1977), p. 110.

[18] See the testimony of Dr. Avigdor Haskelkorn in the *Hearings before the Subcommittee on Near Eastern and South Asian Affairs of the Committee on Foreign Relations,* U.S. Senate, 95th Congress, May 18, 1977, pp. 6-35 for a review of Soviet activity in the Mideast and Persian Gulf regions.

[19] Joseph Churba, *The Politics of Defeat: America's Decline in the Middle East* (New York: Cyrco Press, 1977), p. 200. See also Churba's testimony in Hearings noted in ft. 18, May 20, 1977, pp. 53-72.

[20] For a somewhat positive picture of the *dhimmi,* see Bernard Lewis, *The Arabs in History* (New York: Harper & Row, 1967), pp. 93-4; for a somewhat negative picture, see Gustave E. Von Grunebaum, *Medieval Islam* (Chicago: University of Chicago Press, 1971), pp. 177-85.

[21] Philip J. Baram, *The Department of State in the Middle East, 1919-1945* (University of Pennsylvania Press, 1978), p. 77.

[22] *U.S. News and World Report, op. cit.* p. 37.

[23] G.E. Von Grunebaum, *Islam: Essays in the Nature and Growth of a Cultural Tradition* (London: Routledge & Kegan Paul, 1969), p. 48.

[24] Ray S. Cline, *World Power Assessment: A Calculus of Strategic Drift* (Washington: Georgetown University, The Center for Strategic and International Studies, 1975), pp. 131-33.

[25] See William B. Quandt, "Soviet Policy in the October Middle East War — I," *International Affairs,* July 1977, p. 383; and Eugene V. Rostow, "Can the Tide Be Turned?" in Eugene V. Rostow, ed., *The Middle East: Critical Choices For the United States* (Boulder: Westview, 1976), pp. 20-22.

[26] Uri Ra'anan, "The Soviet-Egyptian 'Rift'," *Commentary,* June 1976, pp. 29-35; and by the same author, "The Soviet Union and the Middle East," in Eugene V. Rostow, ed., *The Middle East: Critical Choices for the United States,* pp. 31-45.

[27] *Senate Delegation Report on American Foreign Policy and Nonproliferation Interests in the Middle East,* Report, June 1977, p. 17.

[28] From a UPI (Beirut) release, as reported in *The Jerusalem Post,* Dec. 19, 1979. Approximately 60 Saudi troops were killed and 200 wounded in the battles against the attackers.

[29] *Newsweek,* Dec. 24, 1979, p. 14.

[30] Henry A. Kissinger, *The Necessity for Choice: Prospects of American Foreign Policy* (Garden City, N.Y.: Doubleday, 1962), pp. 182-217.

CHAPTER 2

[1] The Brookings Institution, *Toward Peace in the Middle East: Report of a Study Group* (Washington, 1975).

[2] "Oil and Turmoil: Western Choices in the Middle East," The Atlantic Council's Special Working Group on

the Middle East, *Atlantic Community Quarterly,* Fall 1979, pp. 291-305.

[3] *Ibid.,* p. 294.

[4] *Ibid.,* pp. 302-03.

[5] *Toward Peace in the Middle East,* p. 11.

[6] *The Department of State in the Middle East,* pp. 10-20, 73-91, and 283-87.

[7] The Letter by over 170 retired American admirals and generals was distributed by *Foreign Policy Perspectives, Inc.,* Boston, dated Dec. 11, 1978.

[8] Various conservative or neo-conservative elements in military, political, and religious circles, as well as parts of the American labor sector, seem to identify with the outlook expressed in the Letter of the generals. We recall that airport service crews refused to handle Soviet civil flights in the U.S. after Carter imposed certain sanctions on the Russians following their massive invasion of Afghanistan.

[9] *Toward Peace in the Middle East,* p. 5.

[10] "Oil and Turmoil," p. 302.

[11] *Toward Peace in the Middle East,* p. 6.

[12] John S. Badeau, *The American Approach to the Arab World* (New York: Harper & Row, 1968), p. 28. Badeau, writing in 1968, does not list oil as one of the basic American interests in the Arab world; 'oil consciousness' is really a part of the era of the 1970s.

[13] George W. Ball, *From Partial Peace to Real Peace,* Address at the 33rd Annual Conference of the Middle East Institute, Washington, Oct. 5, 1979, p. 14.

[14] Governor John B. Connally, Address on the Middle

East before the Washington Press Club, Oct. 11, 1979, pp. 2-3, 9 (printed by Connally for President Headquarters in Washington).

[15] See S. Morris Engel, *With Good Reason: An Introduction to Informal Fallacies* (New York: St. Martin's Press), pp. 91-6. For a pervasive study on the causal linkage of variables, see Morris Rosenberg, *The Logic of Survey Analysis* (New York: Basic Books, 1968).

[16] Alan R. Taylor, "The Euro-Arab Dialogue: Quest for an Interregional Partnership," *Middle East Journal,* Autumn 1978, p. 433.

[17] Mordechai Nisan, "PLO 'Moderates'," *The Jerusalem Quarterly,* Fall 1976, pp. 70-82. The passage of a few years has not altered the conclusion, because there is no new evidence to the contrary, that the PLO is a monolithic body uniformly opposed to Israel's existence.

[18] William B. Quandt, "Political Stability and Instability in the Middle East," Chatham House Conference of 20th June 1979 (The Royal Institute of International Affairs, London), p. 4.

[19] Elie Kedourie, "Misreading the Middle East," *Commentary,* July 1979, p. 38.

[20] Saunders' testimony to Congress was from May 3, 1979. At the end of July he appeared before the House International Relations Committee and again implied that moderation is now coming out of the PLO camp.

[21] John K. Cooley, "Iran, the Palestinians, and the Gulf," *Foreign Affairs,* Summer 1979, pp. 1017-1034.

[22] "Oil and Turmoil," p. 305.

[23] Paul Eidelberg, "Can Israel Save the United States?", *Midstream,* December 1978, pp. 3-9.

[24] From a speech by Loyal Gould, Chairman of the Department of Journalism, Baylor University (Manuscript), p. 4 (1979).

[25] Connally, p. 5. It is not at all clear that Sadat had really cut ties with the Russians. There is good evidence that even after 1972, until at least 1977, Egypt received tanks and planes. See *The New York Times,* April 23, 1978. In 1975 Sadat said that it would take 20 years to replace the USSR as Egypt's major arms supplier.

[26] Eugene V. Rostow, "Can the Tide be Turned?", in his book, *The Middle East: Critical Choices for the United States, op. cit.,* p. 10.

[27] See "Arab Businessmen Tour U.S.," in *PetroImpact: Reports on Growing Arab Involvement In American Affairs,* I, 2 (New York: The American Jewish Committee, June 1978).

[28] *U.S. Arms Policies in the Persian Gulf and Red Sea Areas: Past, Present, and Future.* Report of a Staff Survey Mission to Ethiopia, Iran and the Arabian Peninsula, Dec. 1977 (Washington, 1977), pp. 117-129.

[29] Emile A. Nakhleh, *The United States and Saudi Arabia: A Policy Analysis* (Washington: American Enterprise Institute for Public Policy Research, 1975), p. 3.

[30] John Duke Anthony, "Foreign Policy: The View from Riyadh," *The Wilson Quarterly,* Winter 1979, p. 79.

[31] In the words of the Generals' Letter: 'Soviet imperial objectives appear to include the neutralization of Western Europe, in part by denying it access to critical raw materials; the encirclement of China; and the isolation of the U.S.' See also, Jean François and Branko Lazitch, "Russia's Game," *National Review,* Jan. 25, 1980, pp. 97-8.

[32] Graham made a speech in Washington on Jan. 23, 1979, printed in *Maariv* (Tel Aviv), Feb. 23, 1979.

[33] Cline, *op. cit.,* pp. 133-34.

[34] Eugene Rostow, "Can the Tide be Turned?", *op. cit.,* p. 25.

[35] Alvin J. Cottrell and Thomas H. Moorer, *U.S. Overseas Bases,* The Washington Papers, V, 47 (Washington: Georgetown University, The Center for Strategic and International Studies, 1977), pp. 55-56.

[36] *Ibid.,* p. 29.

[37] *U.S. Arms Policies in the Persian Gulf and the Red Sea Areas, op. cit.,* p. 131.

[38] Nakhleh, p. 41.

[39] *Haolam Hazeh* (Tel Aviv), Jan. 30, 1980.

[40] *PetroImpact, op. cit.,* also Craig Karpel, "Ten Ways To Break OPEC," *The American Zionist,* August-Sept. 1979, pp. 7-9.

[41] *Middle East Peace Prospects, op. cit.,* p. 184.

[42] Friedrich Nietzsche, *The Will To Power,* ed. by Walter Kaufmann (New York: Vintage, 1968), p. 15.

[43] Dankwart A. Rustow, "Oil in the 1980's: A Question of Supply," *The New York Times,* Jan. 6, 1980.

[44] Jude Wanniski, "Oil in Abundance," *Harper's,* October 1979, pp. 26-32.

[45] Morris A. Adelman, "The OPEC Game," *Across the Board,* Jan. 1980, pp. 3-5.

[46] Dankwart Rustow, *op. cit.*

[47] *The Herald Tribune,* July 5, 1979.

[48] *The New York Times,* May 12, 1977. And J.B. Kelly, *Arabia, The Gulf and the West* (London: Weidenfeld & Nicolson, 1980), pp. 387-401.

[49] *Middle East Peace Prospects,* op. cit., p. 186.

[50] S. Fred Singer, "Energy, Security and the World Price of Oil," in Eugene Rostow, ed., p. 92.

[51] Nakhleh, p. 67.

[52] Adelman, p. 4.

[53] *Time,* Dec. 17, 1979, p. 48.

[54] *Middle East Peace Prospects, op. cit.,* p. 207.

CHAPTER 3

[1] Gil Carl AlRoy, *Behind The Middle East Conflict* (New York: G.P. Putnam's Sons, 1975), pp. 94-104.

[2] "Oil and Turmoil," p. 303.

[3] *Middle East Peace Prospects,* p. 315. Kissinger's statement was from April 1976.

[4] Secretary Brown before the House Foreign Affairs Committee, Feb. 19, 1980.

[5] *Middle East Peace Prospects,* p. 3.

[6] Assistant Secretary of State Harold Saunders before the Senate Foreign Relations Committee, March 24, 1980.

[7] Wolf Blitzer, "Adding Up The Aid," *The Jerusalem Post,* Dec. 21, 1979.

[8] From Senator Ribicoff's speech in the Senate on "Middle East Arms Sales', *Congressional Record,* 124, 71, May 15, 1978.

[9] Seymour Martin Lipset and William Schneider, "Carter vs. Israel: What the Polls Reveal," *Commentary,* November 1977, p. 29.

[10] *Toward Peace in the Middle East,* p. 23.

[11] *Ibid.,* p. 21.

[12] Zbigniew Brzezinski, "A Plan for Peace in the Middle East," *The New Leader,* Jan. 7, 1974, p. 9.

[13] General Raphael Eitan, Israel's chief-of-staff, said in an interview for Israel's Independence Day in 1978 that the defense forces 'will not be able to defend the state and protect its independence without Judea and Samaria or the Golan Heights'. This was another way of saying that Israel with a 10 mile width cannot survive.

[14] Butrus Ghali, Egypt's acting Minister of State for Foreign Affajrs since Sadat's visit to Jerusalem in 1977, called for the 'Arabization of Israel' in an interview with a delegation from the American Professors For Peace In The Middle East on June 4, 1975. Only by Arabizing could Israel, Ghali argued, become integrated into the Middle East. Israel's Jewishness — as for Byroade — is rejected as much as the Frenchness of Algeria. The Algerian model, where the 'colonizers' go home, was in fact suggested as a solution by Ghali for Israel during another conversation he had with AAPME on May 30, 1977.

[15] *The American Approach to the Arab World,* pp. 27, 183.

[16] Reported in *Maariv* (Tel Aviv), March 27, 1980.

[17] This point is developed elsewhere by myself in "An Unnatural State," *The Jerusalem Post,* April 22, 1980. It is not irrelevant to quote a statement from Sadat in 1962 when, referring to Israel's narrow lines, he claimed they

were 'ridiculous in the eyes of every man who looks at the world map'.

[18] Steven David, "Realignment in the Horn: The Soviet Advantage," *International Security,* Fall 1979, p. 89 makes reference to this point.

[19] Marvin Kalb and Bernard Kalb, *Kissinger* (New York: Dell, 1975), p. 578.

[20] Cited in Shlomo Slonim, *United States-Israel Relations, 1967-1973: A Study in the Convergence and Divergence of Interests,* Hebrew University of Jerusalem, The Leonard Davis Institute for International Relations (Jerusalem, Sept. 1974), p. 34.

[21] Paul Eidelberg, "Can Israel Save the United States?", *op. cit.,* p. 4.

[22] Testimony submitted by Hon. Stephen J. Solarz to the House Committee on International Relations, August 15, 1977, in *The Prospects for Peace in the Middle East: A Firsthand Report* (Washington: Government Printing Office, 1977), p. 2.

[23] Joseph Churba, "Fallacies in the Pentagon's Anti-Israel Tilt," *The American Zionist,* Jan. 1977, pp. 10-12.

[24] Hans J. Morgenthau, "Facing Mideast Realities," *The New Leader,* April 24, 1978, p. 6.

[25] See the Kalbs' book, *op. cit.,* pp. 226-40, and William B. Quandt, *Decade of Decisions: American Policy Toward the Arab-Israeli Conflict, 1967-1976* (Berkeley, Los Angeles: University of California Press, 1977), pp. 116-117.

[26] Cited in Eidelberg, *op. cit.,* p. 7. Also Keegan's statement to the Senate subcommittee on Near Eastern and South Asian Affairs, Oct. 3, 1977, *op. cit.,* p. 102.

[27] Mordechai Nisan, "The Moment of Truth," *Midstream,* Dec. 1981, pp. 12-17.

[28] Keegan statement to the Senate subcommittee (see ft. 26), p. 114.

[29] Besides many Israeli military views corroborating the defenselessness of the country without Judea and Samaria, Keegan, Churba and other strategic experts in the United States have arrived at the very same conclusion. Professor Morgenthau raised the spectre of Munich in this connection in his article "The Geopolitics of Israel's Survival," in *The New Leader,* Dec. 24, 1973.

[30] Albert Liss, "Israel has reason to be wary," *The Philadelphia Inquirer,* April 18, 1978.

[31] *The Egyptian Gazette* (Cairo), April 16, 1980.

[32] Elmo R. Zumwalt, Jr., "SALT, Detente and the Middle East," in Eugene Rostow, ed., *The Middle East: Critical Choices for the United States, op. cit.,* p. 135.

[33] *The International Herald Tribune,* April 16, 1980.

CHAPTER 4

[1] Alexis de Tocqueville, *Democracy in America,* II (New York: Schocken Books, 1970), Ch. XIII.

[2] Father Daniel Berrigan, "The Middle East: Sane Conduct?" in *The Great Berrigan Debate* published by The Committee on New Alternatives in the Middle East (New York, Jan. 1974), p. 4.

[3] *Ethics of the Fathers,* IV, 1: 'Who is Strong? He who overcomes his impulse'. This is a typical instance of spiritualizing the idea of power that is characteristic of Rabbinic teaching.

[4] *Genesis,* XII, 3.

OTHER WRITINGS BY DR. M. NISAN
RECOMMENDED FOR REFERENCE AND FURTHER READING.
ASK YOUR LIBRARIAN FOR THE ITEMS YOU MISSED.

Middle East & Arab-Israeli Conflict

THE ARAB-ISRAELI CONFLICT: A POLITICAL GUIDE FOR THE PERPLEXED (1978, Special Printing). Union of Orthodox Jewish Congregations of America, 116 E. 27th St., NYC, N.Y. 10016, U.S.A. (originally pub. in Jerusalem, Israel, Mekor Pub., 1977).

HUMAN RIGHTS IN THE ARAB COUNTRIES. *Middle East Review* Special Series, No. 2, 1981. American Academic Association for Peace in the Middle East, 9 E. 40th St., NYC, N.Y. 10016, U.S.A.

DOUBLE-BARRELLED ARAB POWER, *Jewish Chronicle,* May 29, 1981, The Jewish Chronicle, 25 Furnival St., London EC4A 1JT, England.

BIBLICAL POLITICS: THE CONFLICT BETWEEN GOD AND PHARAOH, *International Relations,* May 1974, pp. 479-493. The David Davies Memorial Institute of International Studies, Thorney House, Smith Square, London SW1P 3HF, England.

THE 16th AMERICAN-ISRAEL DIALOGUE, *Congress Monthly,* Nov.-Dec., 1980, pp. 12, 20, 38. American Jewish Congress, 15 E. 84th St., NYC, N.Y. 10028, U.S.A.

Israeli-Egyptian Relations

THE MOMENT OF TRUTH, *Midstream,* Dec. 1981, pp. 12-17. The Theodor Herzl Foundation Inc., 515 Park Ave., NYC, N.Y. 10022, U.S.A.

WHAT PRICE PEACE? *The Canadian Zionist Magazine,* Sept.-Oct., 1979, pp. 4-6, 9. The Canadian Zionist Federation,

1310 Greene Ave., #822, Montreal, Quebec H3Z 2B2, Canada.

AN UNNATURAL STATE, *Jerusalem Post,* April 22, 1980. The Jerusalem Post, Romema, P.O. Box 81, Jerusalem, Israel.

Israel & General Israeli Policy

ISRAELI ARABS: THE MOMENT OF TRUTH, *The Canadian Zionist Magazine,* Jan.-Feb., 1980, pp. 5-7, 24. The Canadian Zionist Federation, 1310 Greene Ave., #822, Montreal, Quebec H3Z 2B2, Canada.

ARAB REFUGEES: A LOOK AT ISRAEL'S POLICY, *Zionism Today,* April 1980, pp. 17-19. The Herut-Revisionist Organization of America, 41 E. 42nd St., NYC, N.Y. 10017, U.S.A.

AN ALTERNATIVE TO SURRENDER, *Jerusalem Post,* June 21, 1979. The Jerusalem Post, Romema, P.O. Box 81, Jerusalem, Israel.

A STRATEGY FOR ISRAEL: CONFRONTATION OR CONCILIATION? *The American Zionist,* May-June, 1976, pp. 19-21. The Zionist Organization of America, ZOA House, 4 E. 34th St., NYC, N.Y. 10016, U.S.A.

THE IDEA OF A JEWISH STATE RECONSIDERED, *Viewpoints,* IX, 3, 1976, pp. 21-25. The Labor Zionist Movement of Canada, 4770 Kent Ave., #300, Montreal, Quebec H3W 1H2, Canada.

ISRAEL FACES THE UNITED STATES, *The Canadian Zionist Magazine,* May 1978, pp. 13-14, 17. The Canadian Zionist Federation, 1310 Greene Ave., #822, Montreal, Quebec H3Z 2B2, Canada.

HARKABI'S DESPAIR, *Midstream,* May 1979, pp. 9-17. The Theodor Herzl Foundation Inc., 515 Park Ave., NYC, N.Y. 10022, U.S.A.

TERRITORIES OR PEACE: A FALSE DICHOTOMY, *Jerusalem Post,* Sept. 26, 1978. The Jerusalem Post, Romema, P.O. Box 81, Jerusalem, Israel.

AMERICA AS PEACEMAKER, *Jerusalem Post,* Sept. 4, 1978. The Jerusalem Post, Romema, P.O. Box 81, Jerusalem, Israel.

STRATEGY FOR LEBANON, *Jerusalem Post,* June 11, 1982. The Jerusalem Post, Romema, P.O. Box 81, Jerusalem, Israel.

Judea-Samaria and 'Palestinian' Issues

ISRAEL AND THE TERRITORIES: A STUDY IN CONTROL, 1917-1977, pub. 1978. Turtledove Pub., P.O. Box 1337, Ramat Gan, Israel.

THE SO-CALLED 'PALESTINIAN ISSUE'. 1982. The Israel Foreign, Ministry, Information Office, Jaffa Road, Jerusalem, Israel.

THE QUESTION OF SETTLEMENTS, *The Israel Economist,* Sept.-Oct., 1979, p. 30. Israel Economist, 6 Hazanovitch St., P.O. Box 7052, Jerusalem Israel.

THE ISRAEL-PALESTINE ANTITHESIS, *Jerusalem Post,* Feb. 3, 1980. The Jerusalem Post, Romema, P.O. Box 81, Jerusalem, Israel.

SETTLEMENTS NO THREAT TO THE ARABS, *Jewish Western Bulletin,* May 1, 1980. The Jewish Western Bulletin, 3268 Heather St., Vancouver, B.C. V5Z 3K5, Canada.

JORDAN AS THE PALESTINIAN ARAB STATE, *The American Zionist,* Feb. 1977, pp. 15-17. The Zionist Organization of America, ZOA House, 4 E. 34th St., NYC, N.Y. 10016, U.S.A.

ISRAEL, JUDEA-SAMARIA AND JORDAN: TOWARDS A SETTLEMENT, *The Canadian Zionist Magazine,* Jan.-Feb. 1978, pp. 15-17. The Canadian Zionist Federation, 1310

Greene Ave., #822, Montreal, Quebec H3Z 2B2, Canada.

GUSH EMUNIM: A RATIONAL PERSPECTIVE, *Forum,* Fall/Winter 1979, pp. 15-23. The World Zionist Organization, Information Dept., P.O. Box 92, Jerusalem, Israel.

JUDEA AND SAMARIA: THE PUZZLE IN ISRAELI POLICY, *Middle East Focus,* Nov. 1980, pp. 13-15. Canadian Academic Foundation for Peace in the Middle East, 60 Bloor St. W., #912, Toronto, Ontario M4W 3B8, Canada.

GUSH EMUNIM AND ISRAEL'S NATIONAL INTEREST, *Viewpoints,* Jan. 1980, pp. 1-6. The Jerusalem Institute For Federal Studies, 12 Hess St., Jerusalem, Israel.

A HERZLIAN ZIONIST MODEL FOR JUDEA AND SAMARIA, *Forum,* Spring/Summer 1981, pp. 85-90. The World Zionist Organization, Information Dept., P.O. Box 92, Jerusalem, Israel.

TOWARDS A GREATER ISRAEL, *Jewish Chronicle,* May 22, 1981. The Jewish Chronicle, 25 Furnival St., London EC4A 1JT, England.

PLO 'MODERATES', *The Jerusalem Quarterly,* Fall 1976, pp. 70-82. Middle East Institute, P.O. Box 4057, Jerusalem, Israel.

PLOWING THROUGH THE FOG COVERING ISSUE OF SETTLEMENT IN JUDEA-SAMARIA, *The Canadian Jewish News,* Aug. 2, 1979. 562 Eglinton Ave. E., Suite 401, Toronto, Ont. M4P 1P1, Canada.

THE PALESTINIAN FEATURES OF JORDAN, July 1982, Compare Notes Series, Dawn Publishing Company Ltd., 17 Anselme Lavigne Blvd., Dollard des Ormeaux, Que. H9A 1N3, Canada; (originally published in *Judea, Samaria, and Gaza: Views on the Present and Future,* American Enterprise Institute, Washington, D.C.).

DATE DUE

DE 1 8 '92			